LEADING A SUCCESSFUL *Life*

LEADING A SUCCESSFUL

Fulfilling Your Destiny
With Lasting Success
And Finishing Well

Willie Yeboah

© *Copyright* 2009 by Willie Yeboah
All rights reserved

LGCC International Publications

First Edition November 2009

Printed in the United States of America

No portion of this publication may be reproduced or transmitted in any form without the written permission of the publisher.

ISBN-13: 978-0-615-33065-5

ISBN-10: 0-615-33065-7

Scripture Quotations

Scripture quotations are taken from the King James, New King James, New International and the Living Bible Versions of the Bible, unless otherwise indicated.

www.leadingasuccessfullife.com
www.willieyeboah.com

Other Books
By Willie Yeboah

* *Courage*

* *God, The Man of God & The People of God*

* *33 Principles to Have Good Relations With People
Revised and Updated*

* *Living Words Volume 1, Poems
New Edition*

Dedication

To my Lord and Savior Jesus Christ:

Lord, I thank you for your grace and mercy, and for all the gifts you have granted me. Thank you for being my Lord and my God.

To everyone who wants to lead a successful life:

I affectionately dedicate this book to everyone who wants to fulfill his/her destiny, with lasting success, and finish well. May God help you.

Acknowledgements

My gratitude goes to all my friends, ministry partners, spiritual mentors, brothers and sisters who have been there for me all these years spiritually, physically, financially and materially. May God bless you and your descendants abundantly.

My appreciation also goes to Mr. Bruce Barbour, former vice-president of Thomas Nelson Publishers and current manager of Literary Management Group, Nashville, Tennessee, USA and Linguistic Betsy Hopkins for their help and advices.

Many thanks to Jewell Parham of J & J Writing Services for her tremendous editorial work on the whole French translated to English manuscript.

TABLE OF CONTENTS

Preface:……………………………………………..xv
Introduction:……………………………………….19
1. Chapter One:
   You Can Become Somebody If You Are A Nobody……23
2. Chapter Two:
   Knowing Your Family Background………………….73
3. Chapter Three:
   Broken Purposes……………………………...……...93
4. Chapter Four:
   The Meaning of Your Life..………...…………….…119
5. Chapter Five:
   The Passion of Being Useful……………………......151
6. Chapter Six:
   Through or With Somebody………………………..175
7. Chapter Seven:
   The Great Instruction………………………………185
8. Conclusion:
   Pass It On…………………...…..……………….…229

PREFACE

I penned the first lines of *Leading a Successful Life* in the French language in 1995. As the years passed, I decided to translate the book in English as well. This was not an easy task due to my busy ministry and work schedule. As a result, I took more years to translate *Leading a Successful Life* from French to English than I took to write it. Thank God, this task finally is completed.

From the time I started to think as a mature person, I discovered that life has meaning, a concept that did not occur to me as a young boy. As I took a closer look, it occurred to me that life is not a simple entity. Rather, life is a mission, serious, real, complex, short, and full of surprises and vanities.

> *Life is a mission, serious, real, complex, short, and full of surprises and vanities.*

Willie Yeboah

PREFACE

Life as pictured in the garden of Eden described in Genesis 2:8-24 is a paradise. In its perfect state, the garden supplied all of man's needs, spiritually and physically. Adam and Eve had no concerns about shelter, food, and cloth. These God provided generously for them. Life was successful for them as long as they were obedient to God.

When Adam and Eve sinned in the garden, mankind became liable to his own life. Since then, mankind has concerned himself with the question, *"How can I make it in life?"* After Adam and Eve's fall, and their exclusion from the Garden of Eden, they had to be concerned with the mundane affairs that God had taken care of heretofore. However, when sin separated Adam and Eve from God, the Father declared, *"In the sweat of your face you will eat bread"* (Genesis 3:19, RSV). Not only did God make work difficult for Adam and Eve, He evicted them from paradise: *"[T]herefore the Lord God sent him forth from the garden of Eden, to till the ground from which he was taken"* (Genesis 3:23, RSV). When God dropped the couple from His direct care, they were left to fend for themselves. Therefore, man has to build and seek success for his life via the potential, talents, gifts, intelligence, knowledge, and wisdom God grants him.

Many people have not built successful lives, not because God does not want it so, but simply because they do not know what life is, nor do they know how to proceed to build a successful existence. I am persuaded that anyone can build and enjoy a successful life. This comes about when a person's will is prompted by his talents, abilities, knowledge, wisdom, and the power of God. When these attributes are in sync, nothing can prevent one from building and enjoying a life earmarked for success.

Willie Yeboah

PREFACE

The measure of a highly favored life is not limited to money, materialism, fame, and respect. It goes beyond these arenas. The focus here is to plan for a level of success that meets one's physical and spiritual needs. Moreover, the focus here is to build success that is lasting, not temporary. There is the level of success that is measured when people meet career goals, personal goals, family goals, and so forth. Then there is the level of success that is realized when people understand their destiny and find happiness in fulfilling their reason for being. Also, one thing is to be successful and another thing after all, is to finish well in life.

> *Also, one thing is to be successful and another thing after all, is to finish well in life.*

In his letter to the Corinthians, Paul talks about various gifts or abilities that have been given to individuals. At the end of a rather lengthy discussion on specific gifts that are manifested in people, Paul ends one portion of his message this way: *"But earnestly desire the higher gifts. And I will show you a more excellent way"* (I Corinthians 12:31, RSV). Meanwhile, David, the king of Israel, expressed contentment and delights in his own life whose instruction and guidance came from God. David concludes Psalms 16 with verse 11 making this declaration: *"You will show me the path of life; in your presence there is fullness of joy, at your right hand are pleasures for evermore."*

Therefore, by the help of the Holy Spirit, my aim for *Leading A Successful Life* is to share with you how you can

PREFACE

build a life in this world in a way that you can have a lasting success and finish well in life. It is my prayer that God shall give you the will, intelligence, ability, wisdom, anointing and capacity to build a successful life that ends well in order to leave a positive impact in this world.

Willie Yeboah

Introduction
LIFE

I fondly remember my life as a little boy living in Kpalime in Togo, West Africa. My late brother Frankie and I were typical boys—rambunctious, noisy, and full of life as we often played, jumped, and shouted. At other times we sang and danced. From time to time, Mother rebuked us for our seeming lack of interest in thinking and doing something more beneficial. Lovingly, yet firmly, and with a scowl on her face she would ask us, *"Don't you have to think about your life?"* She raised her voice an octave or two when asking this question.

    I remember my brother, two years younger, and I laughing every time Mother asked this question. My father found occasions to ask us this same thoughtful pose. Since circumstances had prevented my parents from fulfilling many of

INTRODUCTION

their dreams, they did not want the same for us. So intuitively, they knew to pass on to their children the desire to dream and the wherewithal to begin early making strides to fulfill those dreams.

> *"Don't you have to think about your life?"*

As youngsters, Frankie and I did not know the importance of our parents' questions. I did not understand that they were planting seeds of thought in my mind during those formative years that would have an impact on me for the rest of my life. Now everyday when I awake from sleep I know the importance of their questions.

I pose the same question to you: *Don't you have to think about your life?* Many people are working hard to build lives that fulfill their destiny and lives that are successful and satisfying. However, in so many instances some adults are like children who do not understand the meaning of life and do not know how to fulfill their destiny, with lasting success, and finish well in life. They are guided by their heart, emotion, and eyes—sometimes a fatal combination for building a successful and fulfilled life.

LIFE is a simple four letter word that is mission, serious, real, complex, short, and full of surprises and vanities. It is a house or tower that must be well built in order to supply people with the means to be happy and successful. If one's life is not well structured, then unhappiness and misery usually are the outcomes.

I also believe in the saying *"life is battle"*. God has given man the authority to dominate life, to have control over the

INTRODUCTION

way we live our lives. After God created the world and its creatures, His culminating act was to make mankind. God's choice was to create man to be much like God Himself: *"And God said, 'Let us make man in our image, after our likeness: and let them have dominion__ over all the earth"* (Genesis 1:26, KJV). With such power given to man by God, then life is subdued so that it becomes a slave to man. In order for people to take the rightful position as manager over their lives, they must possess the skills to confront and battle against the vicissitudes of life that threaten to rob us of joy, success, and fulfillment.

As we take on the battle to live wonderful lives, despite the challenges and stumbling blocks that are sure to come, we must look to Christ to lead us in this warfare called life. Followers of Christ have been given the assurance that the world is ours when we look to Jesus: *"Therefore let no man glory in men. For all things are yours; whether__ the world, or life, or death, or things present, or things to come; all are yours; And [you] are Christ's; and Christ is God's"* (I Corinthians 3:21 -22, KJV).

Beloved, LIFE is yours!

You Can Become Somebody If You Are A Nobody

CHAPTER ONE

* *God Does Not Change, but He Can Change You*
* *You Did Not Come Into this World to Remain the Same*
* *Jesus Came Into the World to Change Lives*
* *Moses*
* *Joseph*
* *Reasons You Do Not Change*
* *The Power of the Past*
* *The Price of Purpose*
* *Trying to be Someone Else*

You Can Become Somebody If You Are A Nobody

CHAPTER ONE

"Generations come and generations go, but the earth remains forever. The sun rises and the sun sets and hurries back to where it rises. The wind blows to the south and turns to the north; round and round it goes, ever returning on its course" (Ecclesiastes 1:4-6, NIV).

God Does Not Change, But He Can Change You

In the heavens, on earth, underneath the earth, and below the sea change is possible, natural, inevitable and recurrent. And yet, God Almighty is the one constant. He does not change. He will not pass away. God, who introduced Himself to Moses as *"I AM"* (Exodus 3:14), declares that He is unchangeable. The letter to the Hebrews declares, *"Jesus Christ [is] the same yesterday, and today, and for ever"* (Hebrews 13:8, KJV). This notion is expounded again when Christ says, *"Heaven and earth will pass away, but my words will never pass away"* (Matthew 24:35, NIV).

Eternal God remains the same and His words remain the same because He and His words are one. Yet, His creation and His creatures can be changed. When we are introduced to God in the book of Genesis, we see the Lord busy making changes. He changed the earth that was dark and without form, giving it light and changing formlessness into a triune—heaven, earth, and sea (Genesis 1: 2-9).

> *Eternal God remains the same and His words remain the same because He and His words are one. Yet, His creation and His creatures can be changed.*

The power of God's ability to change the ordinary into the extraordinary is noted again and again in the book of Exodus when God demonstrated sovereignty over a stubborn Pharaoh. God told Moses that He would make him a god to Pharaoh and Aaron a prophet. Before God sent Moses and Aaron to tell Pharaoh to release the children of Israel from slavery, God warned Moses that Pharaoh would not obey. When Pharaoh asked for proof of God's power, Aaron, Moses' brother, threw down his rod (stick) before the ruler of Egypt, and the staff turned into a serpent (Exodus 7:8-9). Each time Pharaoh refused to obey the Lord, God flexed His muscles in a more powerful way, making extraordinary changes in the earth. Thus, working through Moses and Aaron, God changed all the waters of Egypt into blood (Exodus 7:19-21). He changed dust into lice (Exodus 8:16-17). He had Moses to take handfuls of ashes from a furnace to toss into the air toward the heavens. The ashes spread like dust over all of Egypt and changed into an infestation of boils that broke out upon the people and animals throughout the land. God sent a barrage of hail and fire (Exodus 9:23-25) and locust (Exodus 10:12) that changed the face of the land of Egypt, robbing it of all its vegetation. The Lord sent darkness to Egypt for three days which changed the normal pattern of day and night (Exodus 10:22-23). All of these changes were sent to Pharaoh and the Egyptians so that they would know assuredly that there was none like God in all the earth. Moreover, God had a destiny that He wanted the children of Israel to fulfill. He had promised Abraham, Issac, Jacob, and Joseph that the Israelites would be given a land flowing with milk and honey, and the Lord intended for His children to leading successful lives in Canaan.

Furthermore, God used His power to make changes whose purpose was to make life better for the children of Israel. For example, after they emerged from the Red Sea, they found themselves in the wilderness of Shur. It took three days before the Israelites found water in Mara. However, the waters of Mara were bitter. So when the people complained that the waters were bitter, God instructed Moses to cast a certain tree into the waters. Upon following God's instructions, the bitter waters were changed to sweet waters (Exodus 15:22-25). On another occasion, God changed the bad water of a city to good water that would make the land productive and fruitful (II Kings 2:19-22).

Moreover, God changed the almost empty barrel of meal and cruse of oil for a faithful widow who shared all she had with Elijah, the prophet. For three years, she never ran out of meal and oil because God changed her poverty status to one of wealth (I Kings 17:8-16).

When people do not obey God, He will use His power to change their lives as well. In this case the purpose is an attempt to convince people to obey Him. Ahab had to be convinced that God is all-powerful. So the Lord sent Elijah to tell Ahab that for a while there would not be dew neither rain upon the land (I Kings 17:1). So for the space of three and half years, God changed the natural moisture cycle of dew and rain to drought. And when Lot's wife disobeyed God by turning to look back at the destruction of Sodom and Gomorrah when instructions had been given not to look back—God Immediately changed her into a pillar of salt (Genesis 19:17, 26).

Then there are times when God makes changes to show His power to people who either do not know Him or do not consider Him. When Naaman, captain of the army of the king of Syria, was stricken with leprosy, God changed the leper's skin into skin likened unto a little child (II King 5:8-14).

Finally, there are times when God will alter the course of life in answer to one's prayer to Him. God changed His mind about the appointed time of Hezekiah's death when the king of Jerusalem prayed for more time. Upon receiving the news that his sickness was unto death, Hezekiah turned his face to the wall, prayed to God, and wept, saying, *"Remember, O Lord, how I have walked before you faithfully and with wholehearted devotion and have done what is good in your eyes"* (II Kings 20:3, NIV). Upon hearing Hezekiah's plea, God changed His mind and lengthened Hezekiah's life fifteen more years. If God operated these miraculous, noticeable, challenging and undeniable changes in the lives of the aforementioned individuals and groups of people through miracles, signs, wonders, and healing, He will do such marvels in your life also. God can change your life! Jehovah God, the Lord of Host can transform you spiritually, psychologically, physically, materially, financially, and intellectually because He possesses power to change.

If you are nobody, God can make you somebody. Do not think, believe, and accept that your life cannot change. Such thoughts are a curse (a prayer for injury, harm, or misfortune). Conversely, if you think, believe, and accept the notion that your life can change, then your thoughts are a blessing (an act to wishing and declaring, favor and goodness, an empowerment to prosper). The Bible says, "__*Whoever invokes a blessing in the land will do so by the God of truth*" (Isaiah 65:13-16, NIV).

If you are nobody, God can make you somebody. Do not think, believe, and accept that your life cannot change.

You Did Not Come Into this World to Remain the Same

Beloved, you did not come into this world to remain the same. Change is a fact of life. You are born to change and increase in every domain of your life. The fact of the growth experience of an infant in age, stature, strength, and intellect proves that God has created mankind to be transformed. Paul admonishes us thusly: *"And be not conformed* to this world: but be transformed by the renewing of your mind, that you may prove what is that good, and acceptable, and perfect will of God"* (Romans 12:2, KJV).

> *Beloved, you did not come into this world to remain the same.*

You Can Change, Change, and Change!

If you are a sinner, you can change.
If you are possessed with an evil spirit, you can change.
If you are sick, you can change.
If you are infertile, you can change.
If you are poor, you can change.
If you are illiterate, you can change.
If you are single, you can change.
If you are unemployed, you can change.
If you are fearful and timid, you can change.
If you are oppressed, you can change.
If you are selfish, jealous and envious, you can change.
If you are unhappy, you can change.

God Can Transform You

God can transform your ignorance into knowledge.
God can transform your condemnation into justification.
God can transform your uncleanness into cleanness.
God can transform your fear into security.
God can transform your discouragement into courage.
God can transform your weakness into power.

God can transform your despair into hope.
God can transform your foolishness into wisdom.
God can transform your persecutions and war into peace.
God can transform your problems into solutions.
God can transform your failures into victory and success.
God can transform your shame into glory and honor.
God can transform your debts into treasure.
God can transform your hell into paradise.
God can transform your tears into rivers of joy.

Jesus Came Into the World to Change Lives

John's account of Jesus' first miracle, turning water into wine, underscores the fact that Jesus came into the world to change lives.

> *"On the third day a wedding took place at Cana in Galilee.*
> *Jesus' mother was there, and Jesus and his disciples had also been invited to the wedding. When the wine was gone, Jesus' mother said to him, "They have no more wine."*
> *"Dear woman, why do you involve me?" Jesus replied. "My time has not come yet."*
> *His mother said to the servants, "Do whatever He tells you." Nearby stood six stone water jars, the kind used by the Jews for ceremonial washing, each holding from twenty to thirty gallons.*
> *Jesus said to the servants, "Fill the jars with water." So they filled them to the brim.*
> *Then He told them, "Now draw some out and take it to the master of the banquet." They did so, and the master of*

the banquet tasted the water that had been turned into wine. He did not realize where it had come from, though the servants who had drawn the water knew. Then he called the bridegroom aside and said, "Everyone brings out the choice wine first and then the cheaper wine after the guests have had too much to drink; but you have saved the best till now." This', the first of his miraculous signs, Jesus performed in Cana of Galilee. He thus revealed His glory, and His disciples put their faith in Him (John 2:1-11, NIV).

What Can We Learn From Jesus' First Miracle?

The Lord Jesus Christ was thirty (30) years old when He started His earthly ministry. He exercised His ministry for three and half years. The ministry of the Lord Jesus Christ was a powerful ministry of salvation, miracles, healings, signs and wonders (John 3:2; 21: 25; Matthew 21: 18-20; 9: 35-36). Therefore, in three and half years of miraculous ministry, the very first miracle He performed was the transformation of water into wine.

> *The very first miracle He performed was the transformation of water into wine.*

This was the third day that Jesus had been in Galilee for the expressed purpose of revealing Himself as the Lamb of God. The day before the wedding in Cana He had been introduced to His disciples by John the Baptist.
Christ had gained the disciples' attention by making sta-

tements to them that they found puzzling. For example, upon meeting Peter, Christ identified this would-be disciple, calling him by name, telling Peter he was the son of Jonas, changing Peter's name to Cephas, and defining his new name which is interpreted to mean "a stone." Moreover, when Jesus saw Nathanael, the Lord remarked, *"Here is a true Israelite, in whom there is nothing false"* (John 1:47, NIV). Nathanael [sic] was puzzled and asked Jesus how He knew him. Because John the Baptist had talked about the coming Messiah, a reminder to the Jews of what they had read of Moses, Isaiah, and other prophets, the disciples were somewhat prepared to accept Christ and to become His disciples. Consequently, when Christ turned water into the best wine at the marriage in Cana to make known His glorious power, the disciples readily put their faith in Him. At this point, their lives were forever changed.

> *__The disciples readily put their faith in Him.*

Water Has Great Meaning In the Scriptures

Water is a natural element that is crucial in its meanings as they relate to scriptures. Jesus used it as an integral part of His first miracle when He turned water to wine. It is significant for sustaining life. It is the element used by which people are baptized into Christ, a type of rebirth to change lives. I believe Jesus came to the earth to CHANGE LIVES of men and women. No one who ever met Jesus while He was on earth remained the same. Certainly in this moment, no one who meets Jesus now remains the same. Christ came to the earth to transform lives, and He continues to do so as people become acquainted with Him through the Word of God and commit themselves into His hands.

> *No one who ever met Jesus while He was on earth remained the same. Certainly in this moment, no one who meets Jesus now remains the same.*

Jesus came to the earth to change lives. He healed all manner of sickness and disease—those possessed with devils, those which were lunatic, those with palsy (Matthew 4:23-24); He healed Peter's mother-in-law who lay sick with a fever (Matthew 8:14); He healed a man who was near death, the favorite servant of a centurion (Luke 7:2-10); He healed a nobleman's son who was sick at the point of death (John 4:46); He healed the blind (John 9:1-7), and He healed the lame (John 5:2-9).

Jesus raised Lazarus, the brother of Mary and Martha, to life after he had been dead for four days (John 11:2-45). He liberated the captives and the oppressed and healed the broken-hearted (Luke 4:18-19). Jesus' presence in peoples' lives meant a transformation was about to take place. When Jesus confronted people concerning the issues they faced, their lives were forever altered and great transformations occurred. The Bible says, "_the chief priests and the teachers of the law saw the wonderful things He did and the children shouting in the temple area, "Hosanna to the Son of David." (Matthew 21:14-15).

Jesus proclaimed His transforming power by contrasting

thief comes only to steal and kill and destroy; I have come that they [mankind] may have life, and have it to the full" (John 10:10, NIV).

Centuries before the coming of Christ, Hannah, the mother of Samuel prayed a prayer of praise about various transformations the Lord makes in the lives of people: *"The Lord sends poverty and wealth; He humbles and He exalts. He raises the poor from the dust and lifts the needy from the ash heap; He seats them with princes and has them inherit a throne of honor"* (I Samuel 2:4-8, NIV).

Beloved, you can be transformed. God can change every negative thing in your life into a positive. Whatever needs a transformation in your life—your character, attitude, appearance, talents, position, circumstances, health, marriage—God can make it happen.

> *God can change every negative thing in your life into a positive.*

Moses

Moses went from being a fugitive infant floating on the Nile in a basket, to living in the palace of the king of Egypt as a prince, to living as a shepherd in Midian, and to becoming the greatest prophet as a forerunner to Christ.

In the lives of His people, God works wonders. We see examples of this fact time and again as the scriptures unfold. For example, we see how God worked in the lives of two Hebrew midwives, Shiphrah and Puah, when they disobeyed the king who gave them orders to kill all the boy babies born to the Hebrew women. Following Joseph's death, there arose a pharaoh who did not know Joseph or have an allegiance to him. When this new king of Egypt saw how the Hebrews were multiplying, he imagined that someday they would out-number the Egyptians and join forces with enemies to overthrow him and his countrymen. This is the reason he gave orders to Shiphrah and Puah to destroy all the male babies whose birth they assisted. But according to the scriptures, *". . . the midwives feared God, and did not do what the king of Egypt commanded them, but let the male children live"* (Exodus 1:17, RSV).

> *In the lives of His people, God works wonders.*

Obviously God worked in the lives of the midwives because of their obedience to Him. He also worked in the lives of the Hebrew women since they were delivering their babies before the midwives could get to them. When Pharaoh realized the women disobeyed him, he questioned their decision. He summoned the women to him and asked, *"Why have you done this? Why have you let the boys live?"* (Exodus 1:18, NIV). But the women feared God more than they feared the king. They explained to him, *"Sir, the Hebrew women have their babies so quickly that we can't get there in time! They are not slow like the Egyptian women!"* (Exodus 1:19, LB). Disobedience to the king certainly was punishable by death. So it is crystal clear that God worked on two fronts in this situation. One, He allowed the Hebrew women to have quick, uncomplicated deliveries; two, He did not allow the king's murderous spirit to spread to Shiphrah and Puah.

> *But the women feared God more than they feared the king.*

We see God's wondrous power working in the life of another one of his servants—Moses. We are introduced to Moses when he is an infant, during the time when the king of Egypt commanded the death of all boy babies born to Hebrew mothers. As mothers are naturally protective of their children, Jochebed, Moses' mother, kept him hidden for three months before she made a basket designed especially to float on the Nile River with baby Moses inside. Apparently Jochebed had thought and executed a good plan, for when she put the basket into the water, she instructed Moses' sister, Miriam, to see what happened.

Pharaoh's daughter went to the Nile River to bathe at the same time Jochebed put the basket into the water. When the king's daughter noticed the basket floating among the reeds, she sent one of the maids who attended her to go get the basket. When Pharaoh's daughter opened the basket and looked inside, she noticed that the baby belonged to one of the Hebrew women. The baby began to cry, and the Pharaoh's daughter had compassion on him. This is when the account of Moses' life gets really interesting. Keep in mind that Moses' mother had instructed his sister to watch to see what happened to the infant. So when Miriam noticed that the king's daughter was smitten by the child, the story proceeds thusly:

> *Then his [Moses] sister asked the Pharaoh's daughter, "Shall I go and get one of the Hebrew women to nurse the baby for you?"*
> *"Yes, go," she answered. And the girl went and got the baby's mother.*
> *Pharaoh's daughter said to her, "Take this baby and nurse him for me, and I will pay you." So the woman took the baby and nursed him. When the child grew older, Jochebed took Moses to Pharaoh's daughter and he became her son. She [Pharaoh's daughter] named the child Moses, saying, "I drew him out of the water"* (Exodus 2:1-10, NIV).

This was how Moses became a prince of Egypt from his childhood and lived in the palace of the king. By God's power to change lives, Moses went from floating on the Nile like an abandoned child to living in the palace of the greatest king on earth in those days.

However, God was not finished with Moses. There are other changes God brought about in the life of Moses. After living as an Egyptian prince for forty years, Moses had to run for his life after he intervened when he saw an Egyptian beating a Hebrew. Moses could not stand the injustice being done to a fellow countryman, so he killed the Egyptian and hid him in the sand. The next day Moses intervened when he saw two Hebrews having an altercation. When he broke up the fight, one of the men commented, *"Who made you a prince and a judge over us? Do you mean to kill me as you killed the Egyptian?"* (Exodus 2:14, RSV). At this point, Moses realized that the murder he committed the day before was no secret. Upon hearing that Moses had killed an Egyptian, Pharaoh sought to kill his surrogate grandson. Out of fear, Moses escaped to Midian where he spent the next forty years of his life.

God continued to take an active part in the transforming life of Moses. While in exile in Midian, living in this territory proved to be training ground for Moses to grow, to develop, and to ultimately become a great prophet of God, Moses lived the life of a shepherd, became accustomed to living in the desert, and, learned additional religious training from his father-in-law, Jethro, the priest of Midian. Moses' life underwent a great transformation when he went from being a prince in Egypt to a shepherd in Midian. Shepherding was good training to prepare Moses for later when he would lead the children of Israel out of Egypt.

At the appointed time, God made another major transformation in Moses' life. The king of Egypt died and God heard the cry of misery from His people in bondage. An angel of God appeared before Moses in a burning bush—a bush that was on fire but not consumed by the fire. God introduced Himself to Moses, *"I am the God of thy father, the God of Abraham, the God of Isaac, and the God of Jacob"* (Exodus 3:6, KJV). Then God told Moses that He wanted him to lead the Israelites away from their Egyptian taskmasters and to take them into the land of Canaan, a land flowing with milk and honey. What began as God giving instructions to Moses turned into a conversation with the former prince. Moses was so unsure of himself, he did not feel that he could carry out God's mission. Moses presented the Lord with one excuse after another as he tried to convince God that he had chosen the wrong person for this great leadership task.

First, Moses did not think he was a person worthy to appear before one as powerful as the king of Egypt. Second, he told God he did not know what to say if the children of Israel asked him the name of the God of their fathers. Third, Moses told God that the Israelites would not listen to him nor believe that the Lord had appeared to him to send them the message he would be delivering. Next, Moses told God that he was not the man for the job because of his speech problem. Moses said, *"I have never been eloquent, neither in the past nor since you have spoken to your servant. I am slow of speech and tongue"* (Exodus 3:10, NIV). God lectured Moses, reminding him that He [God] has power over one's ability to speak well or not, to hear or be deaf, and to see or be blind. Yet, Moses' lack of self-confidence drove him to make a fervent plea to God, *"O Lord, please send someone else to do it"* (Exodus 3:13, NIV).

When Moses insisted on being reluctant to do the will of God, the former prince turned shepherd invoked God to anger. The Lord had countered all of Moses' excuses telling him what He [God] would do to make everything alright. When Moses questioned his own worthiness to be one to appear before Pharaoh, God told Moses He would be with him. When Moses told God he did not know what to say if the Israelites asked him the name of the God of their fathers, God told him to say His name is "I AM THAT I AM. *"Thus [shall] thou say unto the children of Israel, I AM [has] sent me unto you"* (Exodus 3:14, KJV). When Moses told God that the Israelites would not listen to him or believe him, God demonstrated the power He would give to Moses—turning a rod into a snake, then back again, and turning Moses' hand leprous, then normal again. Moreover, if these two miracles were not enough, God told Moses He would give him the power to turn water he would take out of the river and turn it into blood when he poured it upon dry land. Moses' reluctance to obey God made him give God another excuse. When he told God about his speech problem, God reminded Moses that He knows all about him and solved the issue by giving him Aaron, who spoke well, to speak for him. God would instruct Moses; Moses would pass the instructions to Aaron, and Aaron would deliver God's messages to Pharaoh.

> *When Moses questioned his own worthiness to be one to appear before Pharaoh, God told Moses He would be with him.*

Upon returning to Egypt, Moses' life underwent another change. The timid, reluctant Moses who feared leading the Israelites out of Egypt at God's request emerged as a competent leader after his return. Initially, Aaron did all of the talking before Pharaoh as God instructed him through Moses. However, by the time God had demonstrated His power by turning Moses' rod into a serpent, turning water to blood, and sending the plague of frogs and the plague of flies, Moses summoned his courage to speak before Pharaoh. Moses refused the king when he called for Moses and Aaron and told them to make sacrifices to their God in the land. Moses stated boldly to Pharaoh, *"That won't do! Our sacrifices to God are hated by the Egyptians, and if we do this right here before their eyes, they will kill us. We must take a three-day trip into the wilderness and sacrifice there to Jehovah our God, as he commanded us"* (Exodus 8:25-26, LB).

What a transformation in Moses! The man who was afraid to appear before his own people and Pharaoh had become the spokesman and leader that God selected him to be. Therefore, it is Moses who confronted Pharaoh concerning the plagues of flies, cattle, boils and sores, hail and fire, locusts, darkness, and death of the firstborn. Each time Moses exercised the supernatural working power of God, he was successful beyond belief. In the end, Moses led the children of Israel out of Egypt, leading them to the Promised Land—Canaan.

> *The timid, reluctant Moses who feared leading the Israelites out of Egypt at God's request emerged as a competent leader after his return.*

In short, Moses went from being a fugitive infant floating on the Nile in a basket, to living in the palace of the king of Egypt as a prince, to living as a shepherd in Midian, to becoming the greatest prophet as a forerunner to Christ (Deuteronomy 34: 10-12). What a lesson for us to learn! When we obey God, we can count on leading a successful life, no matter what is our current status or condition.

Joseph

Joseph is another biblical character whose life was transformed at the hand of God. Joseph's life story is interesting for several reasons. Jacob (also known as Israel), his father, had twelve sons, and Joseph was his favorite because he was the son of Rachel, the wife whom Jacob loved dearly and because he was the son of his old age. Rachel died during childbirth just as Benjamin, the last of the twelve sons, was born. Jacob's older sons were the offspring of Leah, his first wife, and two handmaidens, Zilpah and Bilhah. Jacob loved all of his children, but he could not hide the special love he had for Joseph. Joseph's brothers noticed the diference their father made between them and Joseph, especially when Jacob made his young son a coat of many colors.

> *"Now Israel loved Joseph more than all his children, because he was the son of his old age: and he made him a coat of many colors. And when his brethren saw that their father loved him more than all his brethren, they hated him and could not speak peaceably unto him"* (Genesis 37:3-4, KJV).

Joseph was seventeen years old when he dreamed about his destiny that revealed what would occur in his future life. Joseph had two dreams that he told his brothers and father. The first dream revealed to Joseph that he would rise above his brothers and they would bow before him. When he told this dream to his brothers, they hated him for his dreams and for his words (Genesis 37:8 KJV). The second dream revealed to Joseph that his father, mother, and eleven brothers would bow before him. Joseph told this dream to his father and brothers. Not understanding the dream, Jacob rebuked his son, but continued to ponder in his heart what Joseph had said. However, Joseph's brothers were so incensed by the revelation that they became jealous of Joseph and hated him even more.

Little did Joseph know that his life was about to change when his father sent him on a simple errand to check on his brothers who had gone to Shechem to attend to their fahis brothers. However, a man who saw Joseph wandering in the field told him that his brothers had gone to Dothan. Joseph set out to find his brothers who saw him at a distance coming to join them. The brothers had such hatred for Joseph, a hatred that had built over the years, they conspired to kill him. When they saw Joseph coming, they hurriedly made plans to kill him, cast him in a pit, and say some wild animal destroyed him. The oldest of the brothers, Reuben, heard their plan and delivered Joseph out of his brothers' hands. Reuben convinced the brothers not to shed any blood but to cast Joseph into an empty well. Reuben's plan was to rescue his brother from the pit and deliver him safely back to their father.

So when Joseph reached his brothers, they immediately stripped off the coat of many colors that this young son of Jacob wore the coat his father had made for him. Then they cast him into an empty well. Following this mistreatment of Joseph, the brothers sat down to eat. While they ate the brothers noticed a group of Ishmeelites on their way to Egypt to carry spices, balm, and myrrh. Judah conceived the idea to sell Joseph to them. The brothers agreed with the idea. However, before Judah could concoct this deal with the Ishmeelites, a group of Midianites came, drew Joseph out of the well, and sold him to the Ishmeelites for twenty pieces of silver. They took Joseph to Egypt where he was sold to Potiphar, captain of the palace guard of the king of Egypt.

Meanwhile, Reuben went to retrieve Joseph from the well. When he got to the pit, Joseph was not there. Reuben was so stunned, that he rent or tore his clothes out of frustration for the disappearance of his baby brother. As the oldest son, he knew that his father would hold him responsible for Joseph's disappearance.

Reuben returned to his brothers and told them Joseph was not in the pit. The brothers killed a young goat and dipped Joseph's colorful coat in the blood. When they returned home, they asked innocently of their father, *"We found this in the field. Is it Joseph's coat or not?"* (Genesis 37:31-32, LB). Jacob immediately recognized Joseph's coat. The grief-stricken father thought the worst. "Yes," he sobbed, *"it is my son's coat. A wild animal has eaten him. Joseph is without doubt torn in pieces"* (Genesis 37:33, LB). Jacob's sons allowed him to grieve for Joseph a long time. Though Jacobs' sons and daughters attempted to comfort him, Jacob could not be consoled. He mourned and cried for Joseph and said, *"I will die in mourning for my son"* (Genesis 37:35, LB).

Despite all that happened to Joseph, God controlled his life. God had plans for the success of Joseph's life, no matter what happened. When Joseph had his dreams, God was in control. When Joseph's brothers hated him enough to kill him, God put the thought on Reuben's heart not to let his brothers go through with their plan. When the Midianites took Joseph out of the pit and sold him to the Ishmaeelites, God was working on Joseph's behalf. He intended for the outcome of Joseph's life to be successful. And simultaneously, he did not let the young man's brothers profit from him being sold into slavery.

At every turn when it seemed that circumstances could not get any worse for Joseph, the Lord transformed His servant's life otherwise. Joseph became a servant in Potiphar's house, the king's captain of the guard. Potiphar made Joseph the overseer of his house and put all of his possessions in Joseph's care. The Bible says, *"And the Lord was with Joseph, and he was a prosperous man; and he was in the house of his master the Egyptian. And his master saw that the Lord was with him, and that the Lord made all that he did to prosper in his hand"* (Genesis 39:2-3, KJV). Even when Joseph was thrown into prison after Potiphar's wife lied and said he tried to assault her sexually, God saw that Joseph continued to lead a successful life despite his plight. The Bible reminds us, *"But the Lord was with Joseph, and showed him mercy, and gave him favor in the sight of the keeper of the prison"* (Genesis 39:21, KJV). Just as Potiphar had been impressed with Joseph and gave him complete rule over his house and all that he owned, the prison guard did the same. He gave Joseph the authority to be in charge of all the prisoners, and they had to answer to him. Because God was guiding the success of Joseph's life, everything in the prison ran smoothly under his direction.

Joseph's life transitioned again when he became an interpreter of dreams while he ran the prison. The butler and baker of the king were sent to the dungeon when they displeased the king of Egypt. While in prison, both of them had dreams that they told to Joseph who interpreted them correctly. In three days following their dreams Joseph told the butler that he would be restored to his job serving the king, and he told the baker that he would be hanged. When talking to the butler, Joseph asked him to tell the king about him for he had done nothing to be imprisoned. However, when the butler was restored to his position in service to the king, the butler forgot about Joseph. Two years later, the Pharaoh had a dream that he wanted interpreted. It is then that the butler remembered Joseph. The butler told Pharaoh of the incident of a dream that he and the baker had while in prison. He informed Pharaoh that Joseph had interpreted both dreams and they had come true as Joseph had revealed their meaning. Upon hearing this information, Pharaoh sent for Joseph to come and interpret his dream. Before Joseph revealed the interpretation of the king's dream, he glorified God, telling Pharaoh, *"It is not in me [to interpret your dream]: God shall give Pharaoh an answer of peace"* (Genesis 41:16, KJV).

After Joseph interpreted Pharaoh's dream, the king acknowledged Joseph's wisdom and rewarded him, saying, *"Thou shalt be over my house, and according unto thy word shall all my people be ruled: only in the throne will I be greater than thou__ I have set thee over all the land of Egypt"* (Genesis 41:40-41, KJV). In other words, Joseph was second only to the king of Egypt.

> *The king acknowledged Joseph's wisdom and rewarded him.__ Joseph was second only to the king of Egypt.*

In retrospect, Joseph's life underwent great transformations. Though he could not guess what the future held in store for him, he always knew that God was in control. As spectators examining Joseph's life, it is fascinating to have this example of a man of God who could mark successful milestones in his life, even when it appeared as if there was nothing glorious about his existence. Looking back over Joseph's life, we see his life change as he transitioned from being his father's pampered favorite to become his brothers' hated rival and being thrown into a pit by them; he went from being enslaved in Egypt to being the overseer of Potiphar's house, from being thrown into the king's dungeon to rising to become the prime minister of Egypt. What a change! What a success story!

> *Though he could not guess what the future held in store for him, he always knew that God was in control.*

And yet, Joseph's story did not end here. Soon his dreams will come true. A seven year famine brought his family to Egypt in search of food. As prime minister of the country, Joseph had control of all the food that would be sold to persons coming to buy corn. Among the throng of people coming to Egypt were Joseph's brothers. When they finally confronted their brother, the prime minister, they did not recognize him, at first. In the end, they bowed down to him as his dream had foretold years ago. Joseph sent for all of his family and the rest of his dream came true. His parents bowed before him.

Joseph spent the rest of his life in Egypt with his family and had continued satisfaction following his death. Before he took his last breath, Joseph told his brothers, *"God will surely visit you, and bring you out of this land unto the land which he [swore] to Abraham, to Isaac, and to Jacob"* (Genesis 50:24, KJV). Then Joseph made his brothers promise an oath saying, *"God will surely come to your aid, and then you must carry my bones from this place"* (Genesis 50:25, NIV). Following these instructions, Joseph died at one hundred and ten years old. He was embalmed and placed in a coffin in Egypt. Years later when Moses would lead the children of Israel out of Egypt, Moses would remember to carry Joseph's body with them: *"Moses took the bones of Joseph with him because Joseph had made the sons of Israel swear an oath. He* had said, 'God will surely come to your aid, and then you must carry my bones up with you from this place'" (Exodus 13:19, NIV).

There are so many examples of persons in the Bible whose lives went through a great transformation. I could talk about *Esther*, an orphan who rose to become the queen of Persia (Esther 1:1-22 and 2:1-17); *Simon* (Peter), a poor, illiterate fisherman who became an apostle and the chosen one to preach the gospel on the day of Pentecost (Matthew 4:17-20, 16:13-20; Acts 4:13, 2:14-41); *Rahab*, a harlot who saved two men of God, Joshua and Caleb, was converted, became part of the lineage of Christ, and is counted among the faithful (Joshua 2:1-16; Matthew 1:5; Hebrews 11:31), and *Saul* (later named Paul), a persecutor of the church who became the greatest of the apostles (Acts 8:1-3; II Corinthians 11:22-28).

Beloved you can be changed. God can transform your life and make you somebody totally different. Whoever you are, wherever you are, whatever you are going through, whenever you come to God, He can make you the person He created you to be and do what He created you to do. God has the power to make us more than we ever thought we could become and use us for a far greater service in our families, in the church, in our country, and in the world.

Reasons You Do Not Change

1. You do not change maybe because you have not given yourself to God

A person's life may not change and move in the direction of becoming satisfying and successful when the individual refuses to accept the Lord Jesus Christ into his or her life. When you put your life into the hands of God, the author of life, then the beauty of the ordinary life takes a definite turn, thus, making a transformation. The Bible declares, *"Entrust your destiny to the Lord. Trust Him, and He will act [on your behalf]"* (Psalm 37:5).

> *When you put your life into the hands of God, the author of life, then the beauty of the ordinary life takes a definite turn, thus, making a transformation.*

Your life cannot change to reach optimal levels of satisfaction and success without God being the architect of your life. God is a transformer. He alone can transform your circumstances and your life. In fact, if necessary, He can build you a whole new life that will give you a new zest for living and a new identity. Just as Jesus performed a miracle when He turned water into wine in John 2:7-10, He can work a miracle in your life. Do you want your life to be transformed? If so, give it to God.

2. You do not change maybe because you are satisfied with your bad condition

Another reason your life has not been transformed may be this: you have found some satisfaction in your miserable condition. Although Paul teaches us to be content in whatever state we are in (Philippians 4:11), this message has reference to situations that are not ideal when we sometimes have to make sacrifices as Christians. You have to fight the good battle of faith to see that your life gets better day by day, month by month, year by year; and by the abundant grace of God, your life will truly be transformed in the name of Jesus.

If your life falls beneath the privilege that is yours as a child of God, refuse. Say "No!" to any idea that stimulates you to accept your situation as it is at that time. Keep your desire and be resolute to see your life transformed in directions that are pleasing to God. Decide that you will let God transform your family, educational plans, profession, marriage, or any other facet of your life. By the grace and power of God your life can be changed in ways that will astound you and those who know you.

> *If your life falls beneath the privilege that is yours as a child of God, refuse. Say, "No!"__.*

3. You do not change maybe because you do not know God's purpose and plans for your life

The Bible says, *"I know the plans that I have for you, declares the LORD. They are plans for peace and not disaster plans to give you a future filled with hope"* (Jeremiah 29: 11. NIV).

Your life may not have been transformed because you do not know God's purpose and plans for your life. There are persons who discover God's purpose for them early in life, so they begin their journey to success soon after their discovery. Others take a while before they can figure out what God wants them to do because they do not know. For a period of time, some may not know that God has purpose and plans for them. And how do you know the purpose and plans of God for your life? I will tell you in another chapter ahead. But from knowing what God wants to use you to do in your life, family, and the world, you should build on this foundation by looking at your talents, interests, skills, and training to determine what God wants you to do with your life to glorify Him. God acknowledges that He has given spiritual and natural gifts to His children to perform various functions in the church and in the world so that He is glorified (see I Corinthians 12:1-31 and Ephesians 4:11-13). For example, if you are a talented vocalist or instrumentalist, then a part of your responsibility should be a contribution to music. If you are interested in gardening and landscaping, then you should give some of your time and expertise to beautifying the grounds and providing floral arrangements for various occasions. If you are skilled in the use of technology, then lend these skills to your family, church and the world. And if you have been trained in some special area such as nursing or accounting, find ways to use your training to serve people, your family, church and the world. God's plan and purpose for our lives are revealed within our spiritual and natural gifts, talents, interests, skills, and training. I will talk about this in details in another chapter.

> *God's plan and purpose for our lives are revealed within our spiritual and natural gifts, talents, interests, skills, and training.*

4. You do not change maybe because of your disobedience to God

Sometimes people sabotage the change that would take place in their lives because they are disobeying God in some area of their lives. Is there a breach in your relationship to God? Are you the cause of a problem or problems in your marriage? Are you failing to live up to God's standards as a father or mother? Are you failing to act as a Christian should on the job? Do you mismanage the resources God has entrusted in your care?

Understand that when you disobey God in any regard, you cannot attain your full potential, nor can you fully become whom God wants you to be. As long as you fail to become all that God has created you to be and fail to do all that He wants you to do, you may never have real happiness and peace, and certainly not a happiness and peace that will be sustained in the afterlife. If you disobey God, you cannot see your purpose and destiny come to pass, nor will you have a lasting success and a good ending to your life. Do not be fooled by a destiny you reach that is not ordained by God. Success can be both temporary and deceitful. You want to achieve the ideal, that is, to build a successful life, reach a good ending to your life, and to please God in the process.

> *As long as you fail to become all that God has created you to be and fail to do all that He wants you to do, you may never have real happiness and peace, and certainly not a happiness and peace that will be sustained in the afterlife.*

5. You do not change maybe because of your lack of knowledge

Consider the well-known saying, *"Knowledge is power"*. Conversely, lack of knowledge renders you powerless and can bring about destruction. The Old Testament prophet Hosea repeats the words of God to Israel saying, *"My people are destroyed from lack of knowledge"* (Hosea 4:6, NIV). We understand that there is difference between knowledge and wisdom. However, knowledge and wisdom are needed to build a successful life. The Lord wants His people to be also wise. In fact, the Bible is replete with scriptures that focus on wisdom. For example, the wisdom of Solomon (I Kings 3:16-28), the wise man who built his house upon a rock (Matthew 7:24-25), the five wise virgins who took enough oil for their lamps to be ready to meet the bridegroom when he arrived (Matthew 25:1-13), and, among other examples, the description of Paul as a wise master builder due to God's grace. James, the brother of Jesus, instructs, *"If any of you lack wisdom, let him ask of God, that giveth to all men liberally__ and it shall be given him"* (James 1:5, KJV). And Paul exclaims in his letter to the Romans, *"O the depth of the riches both of the wisdom and knowledge of God! [H]ow unsearchable are His judgments, and His ways past finding out!"* (Romans 11:33, KJV).

Often times your lack of wisdom and knowledge will have a negative impact on you if you are attempting to build a successful life. Lack of knowledge is costly, and the lack of it can cost you in so many areas of your life. The absence of wisdom and knowledge can cost you valued relationships between spouses, between parents and children, between friends, between co-workers. Lack of knowledge can transform your life, taking it in directions where you do not want to go. It can cost you peace of mind, financial failure, and spiritual disaster, among other losses.

> *Lack of knowledge is costly, and the lack of it can cost you in so many areas of your life.*

On the other hand, when you open yourself to become knowledgeable the reverse of the aforementioned outcomes can occur. According to various dictionary definitions of the word, knowledge is the truth or facts of life that a person acquires either by experience or by thought. It is the fact or condition of knowing something with familiarity gained through experience or association; it is acquaintance with or the understanding of a science, art or technique; it is the fact or condition of being aware of something, the fact or condition of having information, or the sum of what is known; it is the body of truth, information, and principles acquired by humankind.

To change the course of your life such that you are moving in the direction of success, and managing your life such that the success is lasting, you need to know some truths, get some information, and learn some facts. You have to make plans and devise strategies to take you where you want to go in life. You have to study the world and learn how it operates politically, socially, and financially. You have to understand how to acquire and handle material possessions, how to possess them and not let them possess you. And while you are working to achieve the accoutrements of worldly success, you must also learn how to keep yourself balanced physically, psychologically, and spiritually. You must learn that every action produces an out come—good, bad, or indifferent.

> *__You need to know some truths, get some information, and learn some facts. You have to make plans and devise strategies to take you where you want to go in life.*

The Bible gives you an up-close look at God and show you how He thinks and operates, but it introduces you to Satan and his demons who are ever-present and at work to destroy you if you follow him. The Bible will inform you about how Satan operates and how he is the great deceiver. The Bible will also show you how Satan works to destroy families, cities, regions, countries, and the world.

Much of what you need to know you can acquire on your own by reading and studying the scriptures and seeking knowledge from others. Listen to what others have to say, especially when their comments are in line with the scriptures. You need to avail yourself to have learning experiences by seeking the proper associations with people who know what you are trying to learn, by asking questions, by paying attention, and by being alert. Remember, also, you can always ask God. To reiterate, the scripture says, "*If any of you lack wisdom [and knowledge], let him ask of God.*"

> *Listen to what others have to say, especially when their comments are in line with the scriptures.*

6. You do not change maybe because you have an inferiority complex

Another factor that can prevent your life from being transformed is an inferiority complex. This simply means that you consider yourself "less than" someone else or other people. Feelings of inferiority can originate from a number of sources—your origin, country, parents, family, race, profession, language, lack of education and appearance. Someone may have told you that you are worthless, you are good for nothing, or you will never amount to anything. From whatever the source of your feelings of inferiority, the damage can be devastating. It is a weight that is worn that can be self-defeating and self-destructive.

Precious one, I have a word for you. Know that you are not inferior to any person in this world, especially in the matters of purpose and destiny. For the destiny God has given to you does not know anything about inferiority or superiority. You should not limit yourself or put borders on the destiny God has given you. Do not put inferiority as a barrier or a blockade between you and your destiny. No one is bigger or smaller than you are in this world. Your life can be transformed to reach great heights if you let God be the source of your power and strength.

> *For the destiny God has given to you does not know anything about inferiority or superiority.*

7. You do not change maybe because you believe you are unchangeable

Finally, your life cannot change if you are stuck into thinking that you are unchangeable. Sometimes when people have lived a life of misery for a long time, they feel their lives cannot be transformed. Satan anchors this thought in your mind to block you from reaching the full potential of becoming somebody in life. In a conversation Jesus had with His disciples, He told them that there are some things that are impossible for people to accomplish by themselves, *"but with God all things are possible"* (Matthew 19:26, KJV). God, in His ways of accomplishing your destiny does not consider how long you have been in a bad situation in your life, but He considers the time He uses to deliver you from your miserable condition. Therefore, you need to adopt God's belief in you and His attitude about your life and destiny. It is not too late for you to become who God has created you to be and to do what He has created you to do.

The circumstances of our lives put us on different timetables to accomplish God's goals in our lives. Therefore, you are not unchangeable. You can change. I want you to repeat this statement to yourself: *"I can change, and my life can change"*.

Job is one of the best examples of persons whose life underwent a change. When Satan decided to test Job's faith in God, the devil transformed Job's life miserably. Before Satan unleashed his miseries on Job, the Bible described Job as a *"perfect and upright man"* who respected God and shunned evil. He was spiritually rich because he had God's favor. Job had a wife and ten children—seven sons and three daughters who had a beautiful relationship with one another. He was also a wealthy man, possessing 7,000 sheep, 3,000 camels, 500 yoke of oxen, 500 donkeys, and a large number of servants.

When Satan touched Job's life, his life was greatly transformed. One day one of Job's servants came to tell him that the Sabeans had stolen his oxen and donkeys and killed all the servants, except the one who managed to escape to tell him what happened. While the first servant was still talking to Job, another servant came to tell him more bad news. According to the second servant, a fire from God fell from the sky and burned up all of Job's sheep and all the shepherds that attended them, except the servant who escaped to tell his master what happened. Before this servant could finish his story to Job, a third servant who managed to escape another slaughter came to tell Job that three bands of Chaldeans stole his camels and killed the servants attending them. As this servant delivered his bad news, still another servant came to tell Job the worst news of all. While his children were gathered at their eldest brother's house enjoying one another at a dinner party, a great wind blew down the brother's house and all of Job's children were killed in this natural disaster. Upon hearing this news, Job expressed his feelings of unimaginable grief. He got up, tore his robes, shaved his head, fell to the ground to worship God, and said, *"Naked I came from my mother's womb, and naked I will depart. The Lord gave and the Lord has taken away; may the name of the Lord be praised"* (Job 1:21, NIV). Moreover, after Job endured these hardships and others of evil and pain, Job declared with conviction, *"I know that you can do all things; no plan of yours can be thwarted [prevented]"* (Job 42:2, NIV).

Even in adversity, Job held on to God. Sometimes God will allow us to endure hardships to test our faith in Him. Though Job lost everything, God richly rewarded Job because of his faithfulness. The latter portion of his life was more prosperous than the beginning. *"[T]he Lord gave Job twice as much as he had before"* (Job 42:10, KJV). Therefore, God blessed Job with 14,000 sheep, 6,000 camels, 1,000 yoke of oxen, and 1,000 donkeys. Moreover, the Lord blessed Job with seven more sons and three more daughters. All of his brothers and sisters gathered around him, former friends and acquaintances returned to him bearing gifts of money and gold earrings. In addition, because of Job's faithfulness, God granted him a long life to see his progeny until the fourth generation. Job lived to be 140 years old and saw the birth of his great-great-grandchildren.

The lesson here is no matter how worse things get in your life, always remain faithful to God and He will surely change your life. When we are introduced to Job, he is a wealthy man. However, after he comes through a great trial, he is an even wealthier man. Also, we learn that change is inevitable. Life does not remain the same. However, when God is the center of our lives, He will see that we attain the success He wants us to have in our lives. Though circumstances can cause us to plunge to the lowest depths, God is capable of raising us to the greatest heights. Yes, you can be transformed into a new person!

The Power of the Past

Maybe your past life or experiences are condemning and holding you from moving into a prosperous present and future. The power of the past can really hinder and block your present life and negatively impact your future. When the past is marked by mistakes, foolish decisions, sin, rebellion, and shame, these blights can oppress your spirit and kill your desire to try something new. They can prevent you from forging ahead to create a new existence so that you can build a successful life. Move pass your past and know that each new day presents the opportunity for you to start a new beginning. When you connect with Christ, your life becomes new. As Paul states in his epistle to the Corinthians: *"Therefore, if any man be in Christ, he is a new creature: old things are passed away; behold, all things are become new"* (II Corinthians 5:17, KJV). Peter had a foul mouth; he cursed at the people who asked if he were a disciple of Christ (Mark 14:66-71). But the new creature, the new Peter, boldly and eloquently preached the first Gospel sermon on the day of Pentecost (Acts 2:14-40). The old creature, Saul (whose name was changed to Paul), was a terror to the Lord's Church and gave his consent for the Jews to stone Stephen. Moreover, he led the charge for a great persecution of the Church in Jerusalem (Acts 8:1). But the new creature, Paul, was the person Jesus selected for a special mission. Christ sent Ananias to convert Paul, saying, *"Go! This man is my chosen instrument to carry my name before the Gentiles and their kings and before the people of Israel. I will show him how much he must suffer for my name"* (Acts 9:15-16, NIV). As Jesus converted people, they became new creatures. Jesus sent a message to John the Baptist telling him about the people who were becoming new creatures in Christ—*"the blind see, the lame walk, the lepers are cleansed, the deaf hear, the dead are raised, to the poor the Gospel is preached"* (Luke 7:22, KJV).

> *Move pass your past and know that each new day presents the opportunity for you to start a new beginning.*

Thus, whatever is in your past that is ugly, sinful, corrupt, or unclean is lost to the past. So get your head up; face life with a new heart and energy. Look with a new hope, a hope for the best. You cannot live the rest of your life beating up yourself in condemnation, fear, and shame. When you let Christ become the head of your life, a new day begins. Look to the horizon of your life to see the joy, peace, love, healing, hope, and victory God wants to give you now and in the future. Yesterday is gone; it is not yours anymore. Leave it for God to abolish. Today and tomorrow are yours to explore with God. Beloved, know that with God's help, you can change the dry, empty desert of your life into a cool, nourishing, refreshing oasis.

> *You cannot live the rest of your life beating up yourself in condemnation, fear, and shame.*

The Price of Purpose

Before you evolve into who God wants you to become and do what God wants you to do, there is a price that you must pay. Sometimes the cost calls for you to suffer for a time. You may face difficulties, challenges, and/or oppositions. It is a guarantee that when you begin a righteous walk with the Lord, you will suffer because you become mindful of spiritual rather than earthly things. But the Bible declares, *"If God is for us, who can be against us?"* (Romans 8:31, NIV).

People use a number of expressions to describe what is happening in their lives. Persons make such statements as: "Things are not going well." If it were not for bad luck, I would have no luck at all." "Everything I do comes out a failure." "My life is a mess!" "What else can go wrong?" "Nothing is going right. I give up!" No matter what you call the suffering you are going through now, consider it as the price you are paying for your purpose or for your destiny to be fulfilled.

It is very important to understand that there is a price for every great achievement in life. Often times in order for us to become what God wants us to be and do what God wants us to do, we have to make great sacrifices. Frequently we even have to die to some things. For example, sometimes we have to die to comfort, a life of ease, short cuts, and quick fixes in life in order to reach our destiny. On one occasion Jesus explained this same concept to His disciples. Christ understood that the time was drawing near for His death, when He would be crucified for the sins of the world. In order to save mankind from the wages of sin— death, He would have to pay a great price. Therefore, Jesus told the disciples: *"I tell you the truth, unless a kernel of wheat falls to the ground and dies, it remains only a single seed. But if it dies, it produces many seeds"* (John 12:24, NIV).

> *It is very important to understand that there is a price for every great achievement in life.*

Some of us will have to give up comfort and ease to reach our destinies. Sacrificing comfort and ease may mean leaving the security of home and depart from living close to relatives. It might mean resigning from a job that provides the comfort of security and ease of lifestyle because the job puts you on a path that takes you away from where God wants you to go.

Sometimes short-cuts can be good, but often they are not. Short-cuts can be especially hazardous when people use them to achieve their destiny. The desire to achieve a goal as quickly as possible can lead you to do things that are unconscionable, such as, lying, stealing and cheating; taking a short-cut to achieve your destiny may cause you to commit murder, buy, sell, or use drugs; you may be enticed to do something that results in a prison sentence. Unfortunately, we live in a world that entices and promotes wrong-doing. So unless we are careful, and unless we allow God to guide our lives, we can fall prey to acts that we think will help us to reach our destiny in record time.

So often before we make a purchase, we look for the cheapest price. Most people love a bargain. However, there is not a cheap price to fulfill your purpose in life. There is not an easy way or short-cut to accomplish your destiny. Remember, also, at times the price of an item determines its quality. Therefore, the price you are willing to pay to accomplish your destiny will determine the degree of greatness of your accomplishment. No one wants to suffer. But understand, one way or the other, you will make some kind of sacrifice to realize your destiny.

It is after paying the price that you will see your destiny being fulfilled. To see your destiny, you must die to the sins of the flesh. In one of his epistles, Paul identifies the sins of the flesh as these: *"sexual immorality, impurity and debauchery; idolatry and witchcraft; hatred, discord, jealousy, fits of rage, selfish ambitions, dissensions, factions and envy; drunkenness, orgies, and the like"* (Galatians 5:19, NIV). If you want to become a great man or woman of God, you have to pay a price. The cost of this success is to obey God. As an obedient child of God you will replace the sins of the flesh with actions that are spiritual and pleasing to the Father. You will spend your life reading and studying God's word, praying, fasting, serving God and man in spirit and in truth. You will ensure your spiritual growth by adding to your life the fruits of the spirit: love, joy, peace, longsuffering, gentleness, goodness, faith, meekness, and temperance (Galatians 5:22-23, KJV).

If you want to succeed in reaching your educational goals as you have dreamed, you have to pay the price of attending classes, reading books, and completing assignments. If you have dreamed of becoming a lawyer, you have to handle the rigors of law school. In other words, you have to discipline yourself to study such courses as legal terminology, crime scene investigation, criminal profiling, contract law, and employment law fundamentals. Your destiny as a lawyer will be to obey the laws of the land that do not go against the word of God. Also, you must work within the confines of dignity, honor, and truth for God to be pleased with you in your life as an attorney.

If you want to be the doctor you have dreamed of becoming, pattern yourself after the great physician—Jesus. After investing years of studying, the price to become a doctor, be sure to be caring, compassionate, and to see your patients as human beings and precious members of God's creation. In these ways you will fulfill God's destiny for you.

If you want to become the greatest godly politician you have dreamed about, you have to be willing to pay a price. Sometimes the price will be great. For example, you may lose an election because you take a stance that is unpopular with your voters, but it is the right stance to take in order to please God. Remember, God has given a promise for us to "know": *"And we know that all things work together for good to them that love God, to them who are the called according to his purpose"* (Romans 8:24, KJV). So losing an election is not a death knell to one's political career. In God's time, He sees that we build successful lives through our chosen careers.

If you want to become the business man or woman you have dreamed of being, you have to pay a price. As God's representative in business, you will blaze a trail of success by going against what has become the norm. In other words, your word will be your bond. You will not have deceitful advertising. You will not gouge customers to pay prices that are unreasonable. You will not sell inferior products at superior prices. You will not engage in unfair business practices. Your road to success will be paved with decency, honesty, and fairness.

If your dream is to have a good marriage, there is a price to pay. You cannot always allow your heart to dictate your choice for a mate. Sometimes the heart makes poor decisions about whom to choose for a spouse. The sacrifice you make may be to let go of the beautiful woman or handsome man who makes your heart go pitter-patter. Rather, you must seek the woman or man whom God approves for you. You want to seek someone who is godly, who loves God, and who wants to do His will. A potential husband wants a wife who will listen to Paul's admonition to wives:

"You wives must submit to your husbands' leadership in the same way you submit to the Lord" (Ephesians 5:22, LB). Likewise, a potential wife wants a husband who will listen to Paul's admonition to husbands: *"And you husbands, show the same kind of love to your wives as Christ showed to the church when he died for her"* (Ephesians 5:25, LB). Then Paul summarizes what the marital relationship should be like between husband and wife: *"So again I say, a man must love his wife as a part of himself; and the wife must see to it that she deeply respects her husband—obeying, praising and honoring him"* (Ephesians 5:33, LB).

What Happens When You Finish Paying the Price?

When you finish paying the price for fulfilling God's purpose in your life and for your destiny, great results occur.

1. The glory of your destiny will be visible for the world to see.
2. The world will start to believe you. People who doubted you because of the way you did things and thought you could not make it, will begin to believe you because you are living proof that God will ensure your destiny when you obey Him.
3. You will experience the fulfillments of sorts—the benefits that accompany your profession, peace, joy, success, and the sense of accomplishment. Am I saying that you will not have any problems henceforth? No! However, when challenges come, you will be at a level at which stability and experience sustains you. Your confidence will

not be shaken nor your progress hindered. You can accept challenges without trepidation, knowing that all things work together for good to them that love God.

Gain Strength by Looking at the Lives of Others Who Paid the Price for Building Successful Lives

The Bible is replete with examples of people who paid the price in order to do God's bidding. By making sacrifices and/or ridding themselves of those sins that so easily overtake mankind, men and women of God built successful lives for themselves and simultaneously fulfilled the spiritual purposes God decreed for them. As we briefly look at the lives of some of these people, we cannot help but gain strength from their experiences.

When God called Abram (whose name was changed to Abraham) for the purpose assigned to his life, Abram paid the price by leaving his comfort zone, his home in Haran with his father and other relatives. God instructed him to go to Canaan.

When God showed Joseph his future and destiny in a dream when the boy was just seventeen years old, Joseph learned that he had to pay a price. Before he rose to become the prime minister of Egypt, Joseph paid the price of being hated by his brothers, of being sold into slavery in Egypt by a group of Midianites without his brothers' knowledge of what happened to him. Moreover, when Joseph arrived in Egypt he paid a price when he was lied on by the wife of Potiphar (Joseph's master) and put into prison because of her false accusations (Genesis 37:1-36; 39:1-23).

When the Lord Jesus Christ came on earth to save humanity from sin and hell, from the power of the devil to the power of God, from sickness to healing, from poverty to prosperity, He paid a great price. Christ fasted forty days and forty nights (Luke 4:1-2). He was betrayed by Judas Iscariot (Matthew 26:14-16). He was lied upon by chief priests, elders, all the council, and calling upon false witnesses to testify against Jesus to "justify" putting Him to death (Matthew 26:59-60). Then Jesus was put on trial and falsely charged with blasphemy (Matthew 26:60-66; 27:11-14, 22-25). The Roman governor, Pilate, gave orders for Christ to be beaten (Matthew 27:26), although Pilate admitted that he could find no fault in Jesus. In fact, he washed his hands before the multitude of people who were present at this bogus trial as a symbolic gesture to accompany his comment, *"I am innocent of this man's blood. It is your responsibility!"* (Matthew 27:24, NIV). Jesus was humiliated when the Roman soldiers stripped Him and put a scarlet robe on Him (Matthew 27:28). Then they mocked Him by plaiting a crown of thorns and placing it on His head and by placing a reed to serve as a scepter in His right hand. The soldiers mocked Him further by kneeling before Christ and saying, *"Hail, King of the Jews!"* (Matthew 27:29). Christ continued to pay the price as He endured more humiliation and cruelty. The soldiers spit upon Jesus and took the reed from Him to use it for striking Him on the head. Then they stripped Jesus again and put on His own clothes before taking Him to be crucified (Matthew 27: 30-31). Finally, Christ was carried through the long, arduous, painful ordeal of being crucified (Matthew 27:32-50). Are you ready to go through your trial to build a successful life? If your answer is "yes," you are not far from beginning your journey to fulfill your purpose and destiny. On the other hand, if your answer is "no," then you need not continue reading this book.

Trying to be Someone Else

Over the years, I have heard people make comments saying they want to be like this person or that person. This is fine as long as the person someone wants to be like has attained success through fair and honest practices, and even more so if these people are guided by the tenets of Christianity. There is nothing wrong with letting someone's success inspire you to do what it takes to become who God wants you to be and to do what God wants you to accomplish in this world. While it is favorable for you to admire someone who has attained success, learn from someone who has attained success, and know how someone has become successful, it is dangerous for you to attempt to become that someone on whom you are focused. You want to be true to who you are as a person. After all, you are a unique individual, and God does not intend for you to clone yourself. Though you intend to attain some of the same goals as someone else, you do not want to lose your identity in the process. While you look to another for learning and guidance, your goal should be to maintain the identity that God has given you and to do what God intends for you to accomplish.

> *Though you intend to attain some of the same goals as someone else, you do not want to lose your identity in the process.*

You Have Something Someone Else Does Not Have

Many times we try to look like, talk like, and do things like someone else. It is a natural occurrence that when we admire someone and find ourselves in the company of that individual a lot, we begin to take on the characteristics of that person. Sometimes when we admire certain attributes of another person, such as, his or her natural and spiritual gifts, talents, abilities, capacities, and so forth, we begin to feel less than adequate about ourselves. We fail to see that the same person we admire looks at us with admiration as well. They look at us, like us, and see qualities in us that they wish to possess for themselves.

> *We fail to see that the same person we admire looks at us with admiration as well. They look at us, like us, and see qualities in us that they wish to possess for themselves.*

One of the secrets to building a successful life that lasts to the end is knowing who you have been created by God to be and knowing what you are meant to do in this world. We have to discover our spiritual gifts so that we can use them to glorify God. For example, two disciples of Christ, Peter and John, are described in scripture as being *"unschooled, ordinary men"* (Acts 4:13, NIV), which lets us know that by the world's standard they were not men to be especially admired. However, because they had tapped into their spiritual gifts and used them for the glory of God, people were astonished at what they said and what they did. Peter and John came upon a man who had been lame from birth. He sat at the gate of the temple in Jerusalem begging for money from people who were going inside. When he asked Peter and John for money, Peter responded, *"Silver or gold I do not have, but what I have I give you. In the name of Jesus Christ of Nazareth, walk"* (Acts 3:6, NIV). The Apostle Peter offered an honest and sincere declaration. He did not have silver or gold which some gave the lame man. However, Peter offered something better. He had the power of the Holy Spirit, the supernatural working power of God. When Peter gave the lame man what he had, the lame man walked (Acts 3:7-9).

> *One of the secrets to building a successful life that lasts to the end is knowing who you have been created by God to be and knowing what you are meant to do in this world.*

In life, you may not have what someone else has. Conversely, someone else may not have the same things you have. Your task is to take inventory of the natural and spiritual gifts, talents, skills, know-how and material possessions God has blessed you with and make sure you use all of these in ways that glorify our heavenly Father.

Knowing Your Family Background

CHAPTER TWO

* *Investigating Your Family Background*
* *You May be Like Your Family*
* *Family Background Links*
* *Spiritual Freedom*

Knowing Your Family Background

CHAPTER TWO

One of the important tasks you have to do before building a successful life is to investigate your family background or origin. Unless you know who you are and where you are coming from, every effort to build a successful life that is lasting and to build a life that ends well could be done in vain.

Consider this analogy. Before any dam to provide electricity is built on a river, engineers seek to know the source of that river. They understand that no matter how large or small a body of water is, it is determined by its source. The source has control over the flow of the water. When the source dries up, the river fails to have a sufficient amount of water to generate the electric power the dam is built to produce.

The same concept applies to the person who wants to build a life whose success is perpetual and on-going. You have to survey the sources of your life. Therefore, it is necessary to check your family background to see how you fare spiritually, physically, psychologically, materially, and financially. You have to assess these areas of your life for their strengths and weaknesses. If you discover strengths, this information is to your good. On the other hand, if you discover weaknesses, you can become empowered to improve and/or correct any deficits you discover. Identifying your family background can energize you and put you in a revolutionary frame of mind to make all necessary changes in your life by the help of God. By improving your own life, you can create a domino effect that improves the lives of your children and other descendants of your family for years to come.

> *You have to survey the sources of your life. Therefore, it is necessary to check your family background to see how you fare spiritually, physically, psychologically, materially, and financially.*

Investigating Your Family Background

When I say your family background, I mean your parents,

immediate family members, race, tribe, village, region, country, and continent. Each of these areas influence your life with their combination of good and bad or blessings and curses related to your origin.

If you are a man, check the lives of the male relatives on both the paternal and maternal sides of your family. Note particularly how the lives of these men started, continued, and ended (if some are deceased). If you are a woman, investigate the lives of female relatives on the paternal and maternal sides of your family. Record how did their lives begin, continue, and end (if some are deceased)? Your discoveries will be signs of what possibly can happen to you as you walk along the pathway of life on earth and as you work toward building a successful life and work toward leading a life that will meet with a good end.

The investigation of your family background will guide you to prepare for war against any forces you discover that have had and continue to have a negative impact on the outcome of the well-being of your family. As you engage in your research, it is imperative that you make the following discoveries:

1. Sins that dominate your family.
2. Evil spirits or demons that control and possess your family.
3. Diseases and sicknesses that prevail in your family lineage, health issue (s).
4. Errors, weaknesses, and negative traits that are traced to your family.
5. Character traits.
6. Appearance (look, body).
7. A certain attitude/disposition.

8. A curse
9. Talents, gifts, capacities, abilities, and good traits that are traced to your family.
10. A blessing

You May be Like Your Family

We understand that man entered the world when God created him. For we know that God, the Almighty, is the creator of the world and the creator of all things in it. The Bible confirms God's role as creator: *"All things were made by Him; and without Him was anything made"* (John 1:3, NIV). The book of Genesis itemizes what God made: *"So God created man in His own image, in His image He created him; male and female He created them"* (Genesis 1:27).

After God made Adam and Eve, the first man and woman, He used them to create the channel by which mankind would populate the world. Moreover, since the beginning of time, offspring have been made in the image of their parents and forebearers. There is an old adage, *"Like father, like son."* The counterpart to this adage is *"Like mother, like daughter."* Sometimes when we choose not to be realistic about whom we are, we tend to disbelieve these sayings. It is true, you can be different from your father or mother. But listen, no matter how you try to be different from your parents, there will be some features or attributes that you will have in common with them. The same is true regarding your connection with people with whom you share ethnicity, a community, a country, and family. Close scrutiny will surely reveal there are some features or attributes you will have in common. You resemble your various origins one way or the other whether you accept this fact or not. This is why a person usually becomes, to some degree, his or her origin.

> *It is true, you can be different from your father or mother. But listen, no matter how you try to be different from your parents, there will be some features or attributes that you will have in common with them.*

A case in point is the story of barrenness Abram (later called Abraham) and Sarai (later called Sarah) experienced in life. In Genesis 15: 2 and 16:1, the Bible is clear on the fact that Sarai the wife of Abram had problem conceiving a child, and years later his son, Isaac, married Rebekah, and the couple had the same problem his parents experienced (Genesis 25: 21).

Another example is a mistake that Abram made, and years later his son, Isaac, made the same mistake. Abram and Sarai, his wife, traveled from Canaan to Egypt because of a great famine in the land. However, before they entered the country, Abram told Sarai that the Egyptians will observe that she is a very beautiful woman, and they will ask if Abram is her husband. Because Abram feared that the Egyptians would kill him in order to have Sarai, he told her to tell them she was his sister when they asked about her relationship to Abram (Genesis 12:10 -13).

The Bible does not tell us whether or not Abram ever told Isaac about this event in his life. However, about ninety—seven years later, Isaac, their son and his wife Rebekah found themselves in a similar situation that mirrored the incident that his parents faced in Egypt. There was a famine in the land, but God forbade Isaac to go to Egypt as Abram

Abram had done and as the people were doing at that time. He dwelt in Gerar among the Philistines pretending that Rebekah was his sister instead of his wife. When the king of the Philistines discovered Rebekah's true identity, he questioned Isaac:

> *When the men of that place [Gerar] asked him [Isaac] about his wife, he said, "She is my sister," because he was afraid to say, "She is my wife." He thought, "The men of this place might kill me on account of Rebekah, because she is beautiful." When Isaac had been there a long time, Abimelech king of the Philistines looked down from a window and saw Isaac caressing his wife Rebekah. So Abimelech summoned Isaac and said, "She is really your wife! Why did you say, 'She is my sister'?" Isaac answered him, "Because I thought I might lose my life on account of her."(Genesis 26:7-9, NIV).*

On one hand, there is this sense of amazement that two similar incidents can parallel each other so closely though the situations are separated by almost a century. On the other hand, these incidents show how strong the connections are between members of the same blood line. Isaac's fear of what he thought the Philistines would do to him if they knew Rebekah's identity drove him to echo the same words of his father, *"She is my sister"* (Genesis 26:7; Genesis 12:19, KJV).

Family Background Links

People are intricately connected from a number of perspectives. Every people, nation, country, continent, city, village, race, language, and family have bonds or links which are transferred by blood, spirituality, proximity, or environment from generation to generation, and from parents to children. There are certain tendencies that are passed from generation to generation.

Thus, when we study family traits, we are likely to see any number of transfers from one generation to the next. In fact, there are times when we can follow family traits through several generations.

Because family traits travel through generations, it is not uncommon to notice that members of certain families are plagued with negative issues such as the inability to love; they are choleric, non-flexible, complicated, unfaithful, proud, arrogant, ungrateful, and mean. Conversely, there are other families who exude positive attributes. They wear smiles on their faces; they are compassionate and loving, easy to get along with, faithful, humble, patient, and grateful.

In appearance, families have distinguishable traits. Family members can be tall or short, fat or lean, ordinary and mediocre or beautiful and handsome, robust or weakly, intelligent or slow, talented or void of worthwhile talents. A family's talents can be demonstrated in so many ways. Family members are particularly gifted in the ability . . .

- To lead or direct
- To organize
- To create (to be creative)
- To plan and realize the plan
- To communicate well
- To teach
- To be convincing

- To resolve problems
- To be courageous
- To create relations easily
- To be disciplined
- To do things without fault, to be exact or perfectionist
- To be orderly
- To be artistic
  - to sing well
  - to dance well
  - to act well
  - to speak well
  - to create magnificent handcrafts
- To support others
- To have compassion for others

Families are featured in all kinds of configurations. For instance, some are positioned high in society. Materially speaking, they have all they need. In fact, they have far more than is necessary. Sometimes present-day family members are enjoying the blessings of their ancestors. These blessings come in many forms, via art treasures or jewels, farm land, businesses, real estate, a house, and cash money. In addition, some families enjoy the blessings of a good name that is well-known and respected throughout the community and in society. There are persons who know full well the significance of the scripture that tells us, *"A GOOD name is more desirable than great riches; to be esteemed is better than silver or gold"* (Proverbs 22:1, NIV).

On the other hand, some families fall far below the privileges that earmark other families. Some families are living under curses which their parents or other family members provoked on them by their evil doings. These curses come in a variety of manifestations that result in such outcomes as premature death, untimely death, mental illness and madness, poverty, misery of all sorts, adultery, polygamy, incest, diseases, infirmities, homosexuality, lesbianism, abortions, idolatry, stealing, and much, much more. Sometimes families are possessed by evil spirits or demons, and these can be spirits of magic, witchcraft, and other extensions of the occult. Obviously, they have ignored the scripture or they are not aware that God looks upon persons who engage in these practices as detestable and as an abomination (Deuteronomy 18:10-12).

Spiritual Freedom

Now the pertinent question is this: Can you be delivered from negative generational links? The answer is YES! YES! YES! The Bible says, *"The reason the Son of God appeared was to destroy the devil's work"* (I John 3:8, NIV). The Lord Jesus Christ confirmed, *"The Spirit of the Lord is on me, because he has anointed me to preach good news to the poor. He has sent me to proclaim freedom for the prisoners and recovery of sight for the blind, to release the oppressed"* (Luke 4:18, NIV).

Before I continue, let me make this point clear. You can be delivered from the negative effects of your family background. But first, there is some work on your part that you have to do. Yes, the Bible does say, *"Therefore, if anyone is in Christ, he is a new creation; the old has gone, the new has come"* (II Corinthians 5:17, NIV). Based on this scripture some people and even some Christians believe that a person is automatically set free from adverse familial and generational issues that plague the family when they turn their lives over to God. In other words, they believe persons are set free from the bondages of spiritual, psychological, physical, and moral damage at the very moment they give their lives to Christ. This notion is absolutely false. When you establish a fellowship with the Lord Jesus Christ, God and the Holy Spirit team up with you to do battle against whatever ails you—generational curses, demons, diseases, bad attitudes, and any other problems that exist.

> *You can be delivered from the negative effects of your family background. But first, there is some work on your part that you have to do.*

The teachings of the Bible will give you something you may not have had before—the truth. Even if you have known partial truth, that is not enough. Total truth can be gleaned only from the Word of God. For Jesus on one occasion when speaking to His disciples said, *"If you hold to my teaching, you are really my disciples. Then you will know the truth, and the truth will set you free"* (John 8:31-32, NIV). Real freedom comes in knowing and obeying the Word of God.

Christianity does not wave a magic wand for all of the problems of life to disappear. Rather, Christianity gives you a new attitude and power regarding those problems and instructs you on how to fight against and for relieving yourself of them. When you do battle armed with the Word of God, you are certain to be victorious in the fight. Paul says it best in his letter to the Ephesians. He reminded them that Christians are engaged in a war against Satan. There-

battle:

> *"Finally, be strong in the Lord and in his mighty power. Put on the full armor of God so that you can take your stand against the devil's schemes. For our struggle is not against flesh and blood, but against the rulers, against the authorities, against the powers of this dark world and against the spiritual forces of evil in the heavenly realms. Therefore put on the full armor of God, so that when the day of evil comes, you may be able to stand your ground, and after you have done everything, to stand. Stand firm then, with the belt of truth buckled around your waist, with the breastplate of righteousness in place, and with your feet fitted with the readiness that comes from the gospel of peace. In addition to all this, take up the shield of faith, with which you can extinguish all the flaming arrows of the evil one. Take the helmet of salvation and the sword of the Spirit, which is the word of God"* (Ephesians 6:10-17).

Christianity does not wave a magic wand for all of the problems of life to disappear.

Sins and problems that have been your *nemesis*—no matter what they are—will no longer have their hold on you when you dress for battle by putting on the whole armor of God. So do just that. Put on the armor of God and begin immediately to embrace the great joy that comes with spiritual freedom.

Fight for Your Spiritual Freedom

Thucydides (460-404 BC), an ancient Greek historian and author, has said, *"The bravest are surely those who have the clearest vision of what is before them, glory and danger alike, and yet notwithstanding, go out to meet it."* Through my experience in the ministry, I have discovered that many people do not want to believe or accept the truth concerning the impact the dynamics of the family has on their lives, especially when the dynamics are impacting them negatively. I find, also, that these are persons who are afraid to know, confront, and wage war against the reality that their family has faults; therefore, they cannot free themselves from the shackles of the issues that plague them. They want to leave the matter of repairing family damage to God. Yet, they fail to understand that God's purpose may be for you, the converted Christian, to give the assistance that is needed to your family. Who better can heal the sinful wounds of the family than you who have come to know God and His truth? Therefore, it is important that you lay aside any fears that you may have concerning problems or issues with your family. As a Christian, God through the Holy Spirit equips you with the anointing and capacity you need. I am reminded of the scripture in which Paul tells the Christians in Rome, *"For you did not receive a spirit that makes you a slave again to fear, but you received the Spirit of sonship. And by him we cry, 'Abba, Father'"* (Romans 815, NIV). Thus, as Christians we can call upon our Heavenly Father to assist us in whatever our needs are. As sons and daughters we can look to our Father for support in our efforts to do good in the work that is before us to deliver and heal our family and ourselves from negative family traits. Also, II

KNOWING YOUR FAMILY BACKGROUND

Timothy 1:7 declares, *"For God hath not given us the spirit of fear; but of power, and of love, and of a sound mind"* (KJV).

> *As a Christian, God through the Holy Spirit equips you with the anointing and capacity you need.*

According to English dictionaries, freedom is the quality or state of being free, the absence of necessity, coercion, or constraint in choice or action, liberation from slavery or restraint or liberation from the power of another. Therefore, anything from your family history that puts limitations on how far you can go in every domain of your existence and anything that hinders you from being successful is enslaving you. And if you are enslaved, then your children are enslaved also. Moreover, this state of enslavement is almost certain to be passed to your descendants, as well. If you do not wage a spiritual battle to heal what is broken in you and your family, you will be guilty of perpetuating the same issues for generations to come.

Throughout history and as evidenced in scripture, men have either fought for freedom, or they have fought to defend freedom. Won't you fight for your spiritual freedom? How long are you going to keep committing that sin or those sins which so easily beset you? How long are you going to allow Satan to have control over you? How long are you going to allow that generational disease to prevail in your family lineage? How long are you going to continue to make the same mistakes? When are you going to say, *"I refuse to be the same! Stop the madness of sin and destruction in my family. No more bad attitudes, ruined marriages, strained* and volatile relationships, lying, dishonest practices, selfishness, and all other attitudes and acts that displease the Lord God of heaven. The family curse ends here, in the Name of Jesus!".

> *Therefore, anything from your family history that puts limitations on how far you can go in every domain of your existence and anything that hinders you from being successful is enslaving you.*

Your Duty When You Know Your Family Background

Freedom costs. When you make the decision to be delivered from negative influences and the destruction that are linked to the family, you must be prepared to make some sacrifices. In order to be spiritually free, you have to let go of your pride and ego, believe in God's Word, power, and truth, and make a whole-hearted decision to give God your life. You have to decide that you will follow God's decision and governance of your whole being as you exist spiritually, psychologically, emotionally, and morally. You will have to start exercising self-discipline by the help of the Holy Spirit. Follow the mandates of God with bold faith, believing assuredly what Paul says, *"And we know that all things work together for good to them that love God, to them who are called according to his purpose"* (Romans 8:28, KJV).

> *Freedom costs.*

KNOWING YOUR FAMILY BACKGROUND

Be patient with yourself as you begin this journey to grow spiritually and to help your family rid itself of the generational curses you have identified. Seek spiritual and professional guidance. Talk to a spiritual and anointed minister. Develop relationships with people of faith who have overcome what you are working through. Safeguard your life by replacing thoughts that are bad with good ones and by replacing thoughts of doubt with thoughts of strong faith. You may have to change the people you associate with for persons who live a godly life and for persons whose words and actions daily glorify God in their lives. Read books and watch movies that are inspirational. In short, punctuate your life with God. And in doing so, you elevate yourself, your children, and future generations to becoming sons and daughters of God.

> *Seek spiritual and professional guidance. Talk to a spiritual and anointed minister.*

Prayer and fasting are a combination of practices done in scripture, especially when a great challenge faced the people of God. Certainly these two elements are in order for you to practice because you have a daunting task ahead of you, the task of changing yourself and breaking a family curse. On one occasion even Jesus admitted that there are some things that can be accomplished only through prayer and fasting (Matthew 17:15-21). Therefore, develop a strong prayer life:

- Pray for God to forgive every sin that you and

other members of your family committed knowingly and unknowingly.

- Pray for God to make you a new creature and to give you a mind to let Him reign as Lord of your life.
- Pray for God to give you the spirit to lovingly accept His will as it is manifested in your life.
- Pray for God to perfect every good thing (talents, gifts, blessings) you inherited from your family and to help you make better use of these good things.
- Pray for God to transform every negative trait (attitude, habit, character, lifestyle, curse) into positive attributes in your life and family.

As you develop a strong prayer life, work on developing a life that includes fasting. Fasting should be practiced in the Christian life from time to time. What is fasting? It is abstaining from food or from food and drink for a designated period of time. It is a practiced evidenced in both the Old and New Testament. For example, in the Old Testament we find that such persons as Moses, David, and Elijah fasted. In the New Testament we have examples of Christ, the apostles, and disciples who practiced fasting, especially when they were dealing with serious spiritual matters. Designated periods of fasting noted in scripture lasted half a day, 1 day, 3 days, 7 days, and 40 days. Of course, the 40 day fasts were fasts that were done only by three people— Moses, Elijah, and Jesus, but you can also do it. During the fasting period, schedule times to be more prayerful and talk to God about whatever you are trying to accomplish.

> *Fasting should be practiced in the Christian life from time to time.*

Once the power of God touches you, the Holy Spirit begins to cleanse and transform your life. Know that all changes will not be immediate because some transformations take time. Rest assured, however, that in time the change will be complete if you continue to let the power of God dwell in you richly. As God governs your life, you will experience new dimensions. How do these new dimensions occur?

- You must desire a new life.
- You must state your desire for a new life. For the wise man, Solomon says, *"The tongue has the power of life and death, and those who love it will eat its fruit"* (Proverbs 18:21, NIV).
- You must make the choice of being freed from all bonds and shackles that beset you.
- You must pray fervently and fast often. James 5:16 says, *"The effectual, fervent prayer of a righteous man avail[s] much"* (KJV).
- You must confess your faith and your new position in Christ. *"Therefore, if anyone is in Christ, he is a new creation; the old has gone, the new has come!"* (II Corinthians 5:17).
- You must act in effect of your right to live a new, successful, and happy life in Christ.

May God help you to be delivered from all the negative links from your family background, in the Mighty Name of Jesus the Christ your Savior and Deliverer!

Broken Purposes

CHAPTER THREE

* *Purpose Fighters*
* *How to Rebuild Your Broken Purposes*
* *The Journey to Your Destiny*

Broken Purposes

CHAPTER THREE

In Job 17:11 we read a comment Job made about his life, *"My days have passed, my plans are shattered, and so are the desires of my heart."* The story of Job's plight is well-known among Christians because there are so many ways in which most of us can identify with him. Even unbelievers know about Job and identify with him from time to time because Job's plight is a metaphor for the vicissitudes of life. We have focused on Job earlier in this text, so we know that Job was a righteous man who lived for God and who took good care of his family and neighbors. Job obviously had a vision for his life and expected to see his heart desires fulfilled. When we are introduced to Job, the success of his life was definitely on the right track. However, life had a surprise for him.

> *Job obviously had a vision for his life and expected to see his heart desires fulfilled.*

In a few felled swoops, Job's life transitioned from wealth to poverty, from many servants to few servants, from a full house of children to a house empty of offspring, from good health to misery, and from happiness to untold grief.

Job's misfortune demonstrates the various types of loses people experience in this world. His distress was so great, Job declared: *"If only my anguish could be weighed and all my misery could be placed on the scales! It would surely outweigh the sand of the seas—no wonder my words have been impetuous. The arrows of the Almighty are in me, my spirit drinks in their poison; God's terrors are marshaled against me"* (Job 6:1-4, NIV).

As Job continued to deal with all that happened in his life, he made the statement, *"My days have passed"* (Job 17:11, NIV). What days is he talking about? Job is talking about his days of glory—those days when he enjoyed success, wealth, respect, joy, and peace as he knew them. Because Job was so deeply mired in the misfortunes that had assaulted his life, he did not realize that this phase of his existence was a part of God's purpose for him. His focus was more on the fact that his life had changed and not how this change in his life could glorify God. In other words, Job said, "I will not see my good days anymore. They have all passed. Life is over as I once knew it. As Job continued to lament his loses, he commented, *"[M]y plans are shattered, and so are the desires of my heart"* (Job 17:11, NIV). What plans and heart desires was he talking about? Job was talking about the plans that he had for his life or purpose, his children, and his dream to become who God wanted him to be, and his dream to do what God wanted him to do in this world.

> *His focus was more on the fact that his life has changed and not how this change in his life could glorify God.*

Maybe there are some circumstances that have transpired in your life that have you thinking like Job. When everyday life changes such that nothing is normal to you at the moment, it is easy to think that the days have passed for God's purpose to work in your life. When misfortune and heartache surround you, it is easy to decide that you will not see your plans and your good heart desires accomplished again.

But do not despair. I have good news for you. Do you remember Job's attitude when life for him had become one big catastrophe? What did he do when he received the news of the death of his children? The Bible says:

> *Job got up and tore his robe and shaved his head. Then he fell to the ground in worship and said, "Naked I came*

from my mother's womb, and naked I will depart. The Lord gave and the Lord has taken away; may the name of the Lord be praised." In all this, Job did not sin by charging God with wrongdoing (Job 1:20-22, NIV).

When Job was afflicted with painful boils all over his body, and his wife told him to curse God and die, he responded to her: *"You are talking like a foolish woman. Shall we accept good from God, and not trouble?"* (Job 2:9-10, NIV). Despite all his troubles, Job kept his faith in God and maintained his love for Him. Though Job did not know that Satan was negotiating with God about what was happening in his life, Job's faith in the Lord saw him through a very rough time. In the end, God restored Job's status, doubled his possessions, and allowed him to enjoy success once again. Moreover, we see that Job's life came to a better end. His heart desires came to pass. The Bible clearly summarizes a beautiful second half to Job's life:

[T]he Lord made him [Job] prosperous again and gave him twice as much as he had before. All his brothers and sisters and everyone who had known him before came and ate with him in his house. They comforted and consoled him over all the trouble the Lord had brought upon him, and each one gave him a piece of silver and a gold ring. The Lord blessed the latter part of Job's life more than the first. He had fourteen thousand sheep, six thousand camels, a thousand yoke of oxen, and a thousand donkeys. And he also had seven sons and three daughters. . . . After this Job lived a hundred and forty years; he saw his children and their children to the fourth generation. And he died, old and full of years (Job 42:10-13, 16, NIV).

> *Despite all his troubles, Job kept his faith in God and maintained his love for Him.*

When Job thought the best of life was over for him, God had a new success story waiting for His servant. Job's life was the beginning of a new day and a new chapter. The end of his life was to be filled with abundant blessings.

Like Job, maybe you have some broken dreams. Maybe your education dream is broken; maybe your career dream is broken; maybe your marriage dream is broken; maybe your family dream is broken; maybe your good credit report dream is broken; maybe your dream house dream is broken; maybe your car dream is broken; maybe your dreams for your children are broken. It does not matter what you are going through now; it does not matter that the dreams you have for your life and your heart desires are shattered; it does not matter that everything is falling apart in your life. God can renew your purpose and make success and abundance come to pass by His power and might. God can put all the falling parts of your life, purpose, and destiny together again and make your life exceed your greatest expectations for His glory.

> *God can put all the falling parts of your life, purpose, and destiny together again and make your life exceed your greatest expectations for His glory.*

Notice how the second half of Job's life differed from the

first half. However, you have to do what Job did—trust in God. If you have never put your faith in God, now is the time to do so. If you once trusted God, but your faith has been battered and weakened by the vicissitudes of life, then you need to work to strengthen and renew your faith. Emulate Job. As he was bombarded with one misfortune after another, the Bible says, *"In all this Job sinned not, nor charged God foolishly"* (Job 1:22). Your attitude and faith in God will determine whether or not you win the battle when the challenges of life are raging against you. Will you fail to realize your purpose? Will your plans be disrupted permanently? Will your dreams and heart desires remain broken forever?

> *Your attitude and faith in God will determine whether or not you win the battle when the challenges of life are raging against you.*

Listen, it is alright for your purpose, plans, dreams, heart desires, and destiny to be disrupted. For once you have survived the storms of life, you know who you are and of what you are made. Sometimes it is in the eye of the storm that we learn our greatest lessons. Your hurt, pains, shames, and falls teach lessons that you cannot learn any other way. The man or woman of God knows that downfalls are temporary. As Solomon states in his book of wise sayings, *"[F]or though a righteous man falls seven times, he rises again, but the wicked are brought down by calamity"* (Proverbs 24:16, NIV). Yes, you may fall, but do not be afraid to get up, face life with new or renewed faith, renewed expectations, and renewed energy. If you gain or maintain a strong faith in God and a commitment to do His will, as did Job, you will see the Lord restore your life better than before. Didn't He do this for Job? He will do it for you, also.

> *Your hurt, pains, shames, and falls teach lessons that you cannot learn any other way.*

Maybe your father, mother, or some other family members have or had a dream that is yet to be fulfilled because along the journey of life their dreams were hit by some storms of life. The storms came and the dreams were broken. If you share in such dreams, it is not too late to make them a reality. Take up the baton; get into the race to make those dreams come true. Be encouraged! Don't give up! The God of heaven will help you. The creator of heaven and earth will assist you. Those dreams will come to pass.

> *Take up the baton; get into the race to make those dreams come true.*

Purpose Fighters

I want to talk to you now about disrupters that fight your purpose or cause you not to fulfill your purpose in life. According to the scriptures, we do not always fight against flesh and blood. Sometimes we *"fight against the rulers, against the authorities, against the powers of this dark world, and against the spiritual forces of evil in the heavenly realms"* (Ephesians 6:12, NIV). We have to understand that the devil is the author of evil in this world. Yet, we have to take some responsibilities in order to win against battles that thwart our purposes, plans, dreams, and heart desires. I want to talk to you about some of the weapons the devil uses to fight against your wholesome destiny and against the person God intends for you to become in this world.

> *Yet, we have to take some responsibilities in order to win against battles that thwart our purposes, plans, dreams, and heart desires.*

When we consider the lives of some men who fought against their purpose fighters, we clearly see that some won the battle while others lost. These purpose fighters are so powerful that they can take anyone down, no matter the degree of spirituality, wisdom, or intelligence the person has. A fact of life is this: men fall! Satan is masterful at finding the spot where we are most vulnerable and using our vulnerability against us.

The Flesh

Over the centuries, the flesh has been winning the battle over great men and women from all walks of life. Succumbing to the desires of the flesh in ways that are ungodly has caused them shame and downfall, sometimes permanently destroying their God-given purpose. From time to time, the national and world broadcasts are replete with high-profile people who have felt the sting when the flesh has been satisfied. Preachers, politicians, musicians, actors and actresses, husbands and housewives have been victims of falling into illicit, lustful acts that left such collateral damage as embarrassment and shame, broken hearts, destroyed homes, lost reputations, loss of trust, and untimely deaths among other losses. Satan uses four powerful weapons of the flesh to attack and destroy your attempt to build a successful life that is good to the end. The devil attacks your purpose and destiny with misguided sex, misguided pride, misguided relationships and greed.

> *Over the centuries, the flesh has been winning the battle over great men and women from all walks of life.*

Sex

Sex is a gift of God when it is exercised in accordance to God's Word. However, over the centuries the devil has used sex as a weapon to destroy the fruitful destiny of so many people. Satan uses sexual immorality between men and women and now children to shatter their lives. If you want to build a life that is successful and have lasting success until the end, stay in control of any illicit sexual desires you have. One fall on the slippery slope of immorality can jeopardize and cost you your good name, position, respect, and achievements that you have taken years to build.
This issue of sexual immorality is not a Twenty-First Century phenomenon. This was a serious issue even during biblical times. Samson fell short of his full destiny by becoming involved with the wrong women. Samson's sexual

prowess was his moral weakness. He violated God's law by marrying a Philistine woman (Judges 14:1-3) when God had instructed the Israelites not to marry heathens (Deuteronomy 7:2-4); he violated God's law again when he visited a prostitute in Gaza (Judges 16:1), and again when he lived with Delilah and allowed the seductress to use her sexuality to lure him into telling her the secret of his strength (Judges 16:4-31). After Samson revealed to Delilah that he would lose his strength if he cut his hair, he lost the total fulfillment of God's purpose for his life. One of Jacob's sons, Judah, sinned against God when he had an illicit relationship with his daughter-in-law when she disguised herself as a prostitute (Genesis 38:13-26) to get revenge for a broken promise her father-in-law made to her. Probably the most infamous story of immorality in the Old Testament is David's illicit relationship with Bathsheba that resulted in the death of Uriah, Bathsheba's innocent husband and an unplanned pregnancy (II Samuel 11:1-5).

Sexual immorality is a theme in the New Testament as well. It is a sin that abounds in Herod's life because he is living in an adulterous relationship with his brother's wife. The king's life became mired more deeply in immorality when he allowed himself to be seduced when his wife's daughter danced before him and his guests during his birthday celebration. Between the intoxicating affects of strong drink and the sensuality of the dancer, Herod boldly made an oath to give Herodias' daughter whatever she asked. Having been prompted by her mother, the daughter asked for the head of John the Baptist (Matthew 14:1-11). This is a case in which one immoral act initiates another immoral act and then another. Herod regretted the offer he made to the dancer because he had opened himself up to keeping an oath that cost an innocent man his life. *"The king was [sorry], but because of his oaths and his dinner guests, he ordered that her [Herodias' daughter] request be granted and had John beheaded in the prison"* (Matthew 14:9-10). We see sexual immorality again when a woman was caught in the act of adultery and was brought to Jesus (John 8:1-11). But we learn in this scenario that the sin of immorality can be forgiven if you have already gone that way. Stop it and ask God to forgive you otherwise the devil will use it to destroy your destiny and your good name. You may think you will never be caught, or no one will know. But if you don't stop the day of revelation will come when one way or the other it will come out.

> *Stop it and ask God to forgive you otherwise the devil will use it to destroy your destiny and your good name.*

Pride

Pride is another weapon Satan uses to attack your destiny. Inordinate, that is, excessive self-esteem motivated by too much of the wrong kind of pride can cause you to kill your purpose and bring about your downfall. Excessive pride is often characterized in people who feel that they know everything and in people who do not listen and learn from the wisdom of others. These people tend to disrespect others and discount their worth as fellow human beings. When you develop this attitude, rest assured that you are well on your way to the destruction of your worthwhile destiny.

One way for you to have a lasting success and finish well in life is to have a humble spirit and disposition. Paul instructs us, *"Let nothing be done in ...vainglory; but in lowliness of mind let each esteem other[s] better than themselves"* (Philippians 2:3, KJV). The Bible describes Moses as being *"the meekest man on the face of the earth"* (Numbers 12:3), a disposition that made Moses a precious servant of God. As a result we can trace one successful venture after another that Moses accomplished. His life was successful from start to finish, though with a few glitches in between.

> *One way for you to have a lasting success and finish well in life is to have a humble spirit and disposition.*

Be like Moses. Be humble enough to listen, to accept good advice, and to make use of wise counsel from others. Respect others and weigh their thoughts prayerfully and objectively, for they may have a vision that supersedes yours despite your level of wisdom and intelligence and spirituality.

Relationships

Relationships are good and a very important component when you begin to concentrate on building a successful life. However, you need to be very careful and selective concerning the people that you let into your life. Whereas at this time we are thinking in terms of people who can raise you to the next level in life, we must be mindful that the wrong associations can bring you down and damage your purpose. Bad relationships have led people down the path that leads to drug use and abuse, divorce, debt, prison, shame, and other miscalculated horrors.

However valuable relationships serve to uplift you. These bonds can come from a variety of people—good parents, siblings, relatives from the extended family, Christian brothers and sisters, coworkers, and others. Sometimes you can form a relationship with a stranger who eventually becomes a valuable and valued friend. The relationships we have in our lives are so important that the Bible speaks about them. It cautions us, *"Do not be misled: 'Bad company corrupts good character"* (I Corinthians 15:33, NIV).

> *However, you need to be very careful and selective concerning the people that you let into your life.*

Greed

Greed is a selfish and excessive desire for more of something (this could be money, power, position and many other things) than is needed. Look around the world and review the root of some of the evil doings that are happening and you can tell that some of the causes are greed. The Bible says, *"For from within, out of men's hearts, come evil thoughts, sexual immorality, theft, murder, adultery, greed, malice, deceit, lewdness, envy, slander, arrogance and folly. All these evils come from inside and make a man unclean."* (Mark 7: 21-23). Greed can instigate you to commit numerous sins to obtain the excessive of what you want. A French proverb says, "when all other sins are old, greed still stays young."

The truth is, no matter how much you want of a thing, you will never get to that place of enough, especially if it is all about you or out of selfishness. The more you are trying to feed your greed, the worse your situation of greediness becomes and the more miserable you become because you will surely lack peace, joy and self-esteem. You will also become insecure in all your ways. In reality, your greed becomes your spiritual, physical, and psychological problem or illness. This reminds me of the saying, "A greedy man prepares his own grave." Greed causes failure and death.

> *In reality, your greed becomes your spiritual, physical, and psychological problem or illness.*

Have you ever heard about the fable of The Goose with the Golden Eggs by Aesop? It accounts, a certain man had the good fortune to possess a goose that laid him a golden egg every day. But dissatisfied with so slow an income, and thinking to seize the whole treasure at once, he killed the goose, and cutting her open, found her - just what any other goose would be. The lesson here is, "Much wants more, and loses all." When you want to win or gain too much, you will end up losing all. Greed loses what it has gained.

Greed is one of the devil's weapons to destroy and put an end to the prosperous purpose and destiny God has ordained for you to lead in order to experience fulfillment, peace, joy and security in this world. Therefore, watch out for that in everything you do in fulfilling your purpose and destiny. Did God give you the grace to graduate from school? Use your degree without greed. Did God give you the grace to have a position? Use your position without greed. Did God give you the grace to have power or authority in government? Use your authority without greed. Did God give you the grace to have wealth? Use and manage your wealth without greed. Did God give you the grace to get married? Be in marriage without greed. Keep in mind that you can never feed or satisfy your greed enough, and your greed will never tell you when is enough. In effect, it's your responsibility to know and be contented with what you have. Learn and accept being contented with what you need and have, instead of trying to get all that you want.

> *Keep in mind that you can never feed or satisfy your greed enough, and your greed will never tell you when is enough.*

How to Rebuild Your Broken Purposes

If you study the Bible, you already know that what you do after your purpose and destiny have been broken matters a lot. The Bible is replete with examples of people whose lives have been side-tracked from their original purpose, but they took steps to get their lives back on track and to follow the path of their original purpose. For example, Moses' purpose was broken when fear made him run away from Egypt. Yet his purpose was restored after God sent him through a 40 year period of training in Midian. At the appropriate time God revealed Himself to Moses and convinced him to return to Egypt; the Lord armed him with supernatural working power, especially for this mission

(Exodus 2:11-15).

On the other hand, there are biblical examples of persons whose lives were fractured and whose purposes were broken, and the people's lives were never restored. King Saul is an example. His purpose was broken when he disobeyed God, and it was not restored (I Samuel 15:26-ff).

There is one Bible character who epitomizes the points I want to make regarding some simple steps to take to rebuild your purpose when it has been broken. Read the book of Nehemiah in the Old Testament. It is one of the shortest books of the Bible, so it can be read in a single setting. Reading the account of Nehemiah is appropriate because there was a man of God, the king's cupbearer, who set about the task of rebuilding—in his case, he was determined to rebuild the walls of Jerusalem. When Nehemiah heard about the broken purpose of Jerusalem and the children of Israel, he had several reactions to this bad news:

He wept; he fasted; he prayed; he confessed, and he acted

Nehemiah Wept

Nehemiah wept when his brother told him about the lowly status and shame to which Jerusalem and the children of Israel had fallen (1:4). Weeping is a reaction that comes from feeling deeply about something. Nehemiah wept because he felt the shame of Jerusalem and the remnant people of God who remained there following the fall of Jerusalem to the Babylonians. It is a natural reaction for you to weep and mourn over your broken purposes, dreams, plans, and destiny. These are major components of your life, so give in to the emotional backlash that comes with disappointment and failure. Cry! Moan! Mourn! It is difficult to work toward the restoration of the broken pieces of your life if you do not feel the seriousness of the situation. But keep in mind, you cannot cry and mourn indefinitely. Give in to your catharsis of tears for a short time. Then make plans to get up and start to rebuild your life with the same fervor as Nehemiah when he began the task of rebuilding the Jerusalem wall.

> *It is difficult to work toward the restoration of the broken pieces of your life if you do not feel the seriousness of the situation. But keep in mind, you cannot cry and mourn indefinitely.*

Nehemiah Fasted

Upon hearing the disconcerting news about Jerusalem and the remaining Israelites, Nehemiah fasted. The situation was so serious that Nehemiah felt the need to make self-sacrifice a priority. He drew upon personal discipline and self-control to give himself to a period of fasting, that is, extreme limitation of food and/or drink (partial fast) or eating and drinking nothing by mouth (total fast). [I will address the subject of fasting more thoroughly later.] Nehemiah had been fasting for about four months (1:4; 2:1) when the king of Persia noticed a change in the cupbearer's appearance (2:2).

The point I wish to emphasize here is that you need to exercise discipline to restore what is broken in your life. Also, you need to demonstrate discipline in key areas of your day-to-day living, whether regarding your attitude, character, profession, money management, study, worship, relationships, and any other area that needs repairing or a major overhaul. Learn to make good choices about where to go, at what time to go, the reason to go, what to do, where, and with whom. Throughout the Bible there are examples of successful men who have disciplined themselves—Noah, Abraham, Isaac, Jacob, Joseph, Moses, Peter, James, John, and, of course, Jesus Christ.

> *The point I wish to emphasize here is that you need to exercise discipline to restore what is broken in your life.*

Nehemiah Prayed

The third response from Nehemiah when he learned about the desecration of Jerusalem and the shame of the Israelites was to pray. One of the ways to purpose restoration in your life is through prayer. Nehemiah prayed one of the most fervent prayers to the Lord God of heaven recorded in scripture.

> *One of the ways to purpose restoration in your life is through prayer.*

He opened his prayer to God with a salutation that acknowledged the magnificence of God: *"O Lord, God of heaven, the great and awesome God"* (1:5, NIV). When you falter, fall, or lose your way to building a successful life, it is important that you know who God is and understand His power as Nehemiah did. Sometimes your circumstances will be such that only God can pick up the remnants of your life and sew them into a meaningful garment.

The king's cupbearer, for so was Nehemiah's position in the palace of Shushan, was so focused on his request to God that he prefaced the salutation with a declaration that told God that he was begging his request: *"I beseech thee"* (1:5, KJV). There are times when it is appropriate to beg God for what we need or want. When the successful life that you have built begins to crumble, or when you look to see that the successes you have achieved in life have been completely destroyed, you may need to beg for several requests. You may need to beg God to help you keep your faith; you may need to make a plea for the Lord to forgive you of some sin that helped to engineer your downfall; you may need to beseech God to give you patience; you may need to beg God's help to restore your good name.

Nehemiah's prayer proves that he had more than a passing acquaintance with God. He knew that God keeps His promises. He refers to Him as God *"who keeps his covenant of love with those who love Him and obey his commands"* (1:5, NIV). At all times we need more than a passing acquaintance with God, and, most assuredly, we need more than a casual relationship with Him when we are in trouble. Nehemiah's comment is a near direct quotation of Moses, *"Know therefore that the LORD your God is God; He is the faithful God, keeping his commandment of love to thousands of generations of those who love Him and keep His commands"* (Deuteronomy 7:9, NIV). In other words, Nehemiah was calling upon the Lord to be faithful to those Israelites who had been loyal to Him. It is so much easier to pray to God when you have been faithful to Him in your words and deeds. Nehemiah wanted God's full attention before he made his request: *"[L]et your ear be attentive and your eyes open to hear the prayer your servant is praying before you day and night for your servants, the people of Israel"* (1:6, NIV). When circumstances are especially crucial for you or the people for whom you are praying, you want God's undivided attention, and when your purpose is fractured or broken, you want God's full attention when you talk to Him.

Nehemiah Confessed

Next, Nehemiah made a confession to God: *"I confess the sins of the Israelites, including myself and my father's house, have committed against you. We have acted very wickedly toward you. We have not obeyed the commands, decrees and laws you gave your servant Moses"* (6-7, NIV). When you are asking God's help to build a successful life, a part of your prayer may need to be a confession of your sins. If you know that a part of your downfall is related to sin in your life, then it is necessary to clean up that sin. Nehemiah was obviously a faithful servant to God, but he realized some deficits in his life, in his father's house, and in the life of other Israelites who served God. He admitted that they had not been vigilant about keeping all of the laws that God had given to Moses to give to the Israelites.

> *If you know that a part of your downfall is related to sin in your life, then it is necessary to clean up that sin.*

It is noteworthy that Nehemiah knew God's law well enough to know that the people had sinned. This teaches us a lesson. We should know God's law well enough so that we are aware of when we sin. You cannot build a life with lasting success if your life is cloaked in iniquity.

Nehemiah's confession teaches that you should recognize the mistakes that led to the breaking of your purpose. This is not self-condemnation. Rather it is recognition of errors committed that led to your current situation. If you do not identify your mistakes, you will not be able to confront, correct, and avoid making the same errors again. Nor will you be able to properly teach others who will come to you seeking advice.

There is another confession that you should make—the confession of positive attributes that you recognize about yourself. It is necessary for you to verbalize your position, that is, where you stand in your family, at the workplace, in your church, in the community, in the world. And in relation to all of these, you should acknowledge what God has sent you to do in this world as it relates to who you are in Christ Jesus. It is important for you to verbalize this information aloud to yourself because the Bible declares, *"The tongue has the power of life and death, and those who love it will eat its fruit"* (Proverbs 18:21, NIV). Once you make these confessions, you are empowered to reverse the plan and expectations the devil has for your life. Declare that you are not a loser; you are not a failure; you are not a quitter; you are not bitter; you are not confused, and you are not dejected. You are not the tail, but you are the confident, competent, enthusiastic head of your life, taking your orders from Christ who will certainly lead you to build a successful life whose success and well-being will last throughout your days and the generations to come.

Nehemiah Acted

After Nehemiah cried and mourned, fasted, prayed, and confessed everyone's sin, he acted. He got permission from the king to go to Jerusalem (2:4-8); he went to Jerusalem and during the night he secretly surveyed the wall that surrounded the city (2:11-15); he convened the priests and nobles who inhabited the city and convinced them to join him in rebuilding the wall (2:17-18; 3:1-32); he rebuilt the wall (6:15); he safeguarded the city by appointing gate-keepers and guards and explaining their duties and responsibilities to them (7:1-3); he registered the Jews who had been exiled in Babylon and who returned to Jerusalem, allocating their settlement according to family and territory given to each tribe (7:4-6); he had Ezra to read the scriptures to the people and reinstated the law of Moses in the lives of the people living in Jerusalem (8:1-ff); he dedicated the wall of Jerusalem with much pomp and circumstance (12:27-43). This was quite a plan! However, in the end, Nehemiah worked his plan, he successfully completed his mission to restore the Jerusalem wall and the people of the city to their former glory.

The lesson for us is the same. After you cry and mourn, fast, pray, and confess your sin (if you have indeed committed sin), you act. You cannot sit down, do nothing about your situation, and expect your broken purposes to be restored. Something has to be done about your situation.

You have to act now. But do not act haphazardly. You must form a plan. Keep in mind that Nehemiah listened to the message God put on his heart, so his plan was well thought out and followed methodically. You must follow the same ritual when your purpose has been broken and you want to make it right again. Listen to God's message to you, and follow what He says explicitly.

> *You cannot sit down, do nothing about your situation, and expect your broken purposes to be restored. Something has to be done about your situation.*

The Journey to Your Destiny

A journey is travel from one place to another. It starts with a departure and ends with an arrival. The itinerary is the route between departure and arrival and can determine the duration of your journey. There is a journey to your destiny which started the day you were born. The time it takes for you to reach your destiny may be longer or shorter than you think. In other words, it may take years longer or fewer years before you fulfill your destiny. Nevertheless, you will arrive at the intended destination if you remain true to the person you are created to be, if you hold on to the promises of God, and if you do what is right. There will be periods of time when it will appear that circumstances are not working for your good. Remember Joseph. He did not know that when he was sold into slavery and sentenced to prison that God was using these incidents for his good. Never become discouraged to the point that you decide to discontinue the journey to your purpose and destination. Whatever happens, continue to do your best. When disappointment comes, sometimes the answer is simple. It may be that the time is not right for you. Remember what Jesus told His mother before His first public miracle in Cana of Galilee. They were attending a wedding when the host ran out of wine. Jesus' mother, Mary, told Him that the wine had run out, He responded, *"My time has not yet come"* (John 2:1-4). So at times when disappointment interrupts your plans, just know, your time has not yet come. When your time comes, nothing can stop you becoming who God has created you to be, and do what God has created you to do.

> *The time it takes for you to reach your destiny may be longer or shorter than you think.*

Directions to Your Destination

What seems to be non-progress or slow moving to your destination can cause you to become discouraged and feel doubt about the will of God for your life. At times, you are not moving forward because God is using this period to prepare you for the great accomplishments He wants to work in your life. On the other hand, it may be that you do not have the map that shows you the route for reaching your destiny. The map answers the question: *"How do I travel to my destiny? How do I fulfill my destiny?* The answer: pray about your life journey and ask God to reveal the itinerary to you. Talk to godly people who have done or are doing similar things God has called or created you to do. They can give you sage advice and right answers to questions and show you how you can reach your destiny.

> *The map answers the question: "How do I travel to my destiny? How do I fulfill my destiny?*

The Meaning Of Your Life

CHAPTER FOUR

* *Don't Worry, be Concerned*
* *You Are Who You Are*
* *How Can You Know Your Destiny*
* *Your Duty: Bring Your Destiny to Fruition*
* *The Power of Success*

The Meaning Of Your Life

CHAPTER FOUR

How many people are misguided by life in our current world just because they do not know the meaning of their lives? They do not know what they are doing, nor do they know where their lives are leading them. I have heard people make the comment, *"There is no reason for living."* Living without meaning is unfortunate, but living with worry for destiny is also miserable.

Imagine this. You are perplexed and your life is in total disarray continually. You cannot sleep, eat and drink. Laughter does not occur very much in your life because you are worried about your destiny. Precious one, it is true that your life looks like it does not have any sense to it. It appears that you do not have any reason for living. Listen, do not ignore that your situation or problem even gives your life meaning. Your problem actually exposes a reality of life, and there is a reason for your existence and your ultimate destiny. God has not sent you on earth without reason. Surely, your life has a meaning.

> *Listen, do not ignore that your situation or problem even gives your life meaning.*

Don't Worry, be Concerned

No matter what your life circumstances, we have been given a charge not to worry. The Lord Jesus Christ declares: *"Therefore I tell you, do not worry about your life, what you will eat or drink; or about your body, what you will wear. Is it not life more important than food, and the body more important than clothes"* (Matthew 6: 25, NIV)? Keep in mind there is a difference between *"worry"* and *"concern."* Often times there are visible, outward signs of worry—tearing at your hair, biting your nails, shaking your leg and/or foot, or disturbing something repeatedly. However, concern is demonstrated differently. To concern is to relate to, to bear on, to have an influence on, to engage in, to become involved in, to care. Therefore, when the Lord Jesus says do not worry about your life or destiny, He means to control the manifestations of worry. To do this, you must get your worry under control, in fact, rid yourself of any worry. Jesus does not say not to be concerned. Let not your heart be troubled for what you will become in life. You have the responsibility to think soberly, plan carefully, act deliberately, and share in the responsibility of your destiny. As you take these steps, do them with a merry heart rather than doubt and anxiety. The scripture declares, *"An anxious heart weighs a man [or woman] down..."* Proverb 12:25.

> *Keep in mind there is a difference between "worry" and "concern."*

Yes, when you are extremely anxious or have an extreme uneasiness of mind or brooding fear about some contingency for your life and/or destiny, you are destroying yourself spiritually, psychologically, and physically. Again, I am not saying you should not think, plan, act, and share in the outcome of your destiny. As you take these steps, do not be anxious and do not worry. The results of these two negative feelings—anxiety and worry—are manifested in a series of negative consequences:

1. Discouragement
2. Illness
3. Death
4. The desire to do your own will—not God's will
5. Spiritual drowsiness

Discouragement

It is understandable how you can become worried about

your destiny. Sometimes life takes turns that give you a series of negative experiences. When you consider your failures, non-progress, unfulfilled dreams and seemingly unanswered prayers in your life, the first response you have is discouragement. Discouragement is one of the instruments of the devil. Satan uses discouragement to prevent you from moving forward and to prevent you from doing what is necessary to be successful in life. Discourage is one of the devil's attack strategies he uses to cause you to miss your destiny and the plan and purpose God has for your life.

> *Satan uses discouragement to prevent you from moving forward and to prevent you from doing what is necessary to be successful in life.*

Why does Satan bring discouragement into your life? Because he knows that when you are discouraged your morale is crippled, and when this happens you are less likely to move in a direction that is spiritually, physically, and emotionally positive for you. When you become stifled in these areas of your life, you will not realize the full potential God has in store for you. For the person who is usually spiritual, discouragement can cause you to neglect your spiritual routine. You falter in your ability to pray; you give up the discipline of fasting; you neglect reading the Word of God for the reminders of the Lord's promises and the inspiration that is able to sustain you. Discouragement affects other areas of your life as well. It prevents you from optimal performance on your job, in school, accomplishing specialize training, developing your talent, and performing other activities that God will eventually use to accomplish your destiny and to fulfill His purpose in your life and in this world. If you abandon God's purpose, you will fall far beneath the privileges and blessings that only He can give you. If you want the fulfillment of all that God has in store for you, then do not be discouraged. Set your sights on obeying God and doing His will. In turn, the Heavenly Father will direct your path and surely make your destiny to shine like the sun. The world will see God's glory shining through you, and you, of course, will honor God through your spirit-filled life.

> *If you abandon God's purpose, you will fall far beneath the privileges and blessings that only He can give you.*

Illness

Many people contract physical and psychological illnesses by worrying too much about what their life will be like tomorrow. Extreme and prolonged worry manifests itself into a plethora of diseases. Medical evidence confirms that extreme and prolonged worry brings on such illnesses as hypertension (high blood pressure), cancer, mental illnesses, heart palpitations, headaches, skin rashes, fatigue, and obesity, among other medical concerns. One thing is real—your worry will not change anything about your destiny or give a solution to your current situation. The solution comes from obedience, constant prayer and action.

Death

There are untold numbers of people who have committed suicide because they believed, "I'm tired of life. It will not get better. I have no reason to live. My life has no meaning." In fact, there are times when the vicissitudes of life seem to tumble in on us, much like what happened to Job when he lost almost all that he had. In four different messages delivered to Job from four different servants, Job learned that he lost most of his servants, all of his cattle (sheep, camels, oxen, donkeys), and all of his children (7 sons and 3 daughters). Before Job could recover from one report of bad news, he was regaled with more bad news. However, despite Job's financial losses and pain that came from losing all of his children, committing suicide was never an option for him. Even when his wife suggested death as a way out of his misery, Job's response was this: *"Naked I came from my mother's womb, and naked I will depart. The Lord gave and the Lord has taken away; may the name of the Lord be praised"* (Job 1:21, NIV).

King David, also, had a period in his life when the winds of change impacted his life tragically. On one occasion he pours his heart out to God and told Him about princes who sit together to talk against him to slander his name; David admits that his soul is weary with sorrow. Also, David confesses, *"I am laid low in the dust"* (Psalm 119:25, NIV). In biblical terminology, the word "dust" symbolizes "death." The first mention of dust in the scriptures is found in Genesis 2:7: *"And the Lord formed man of the dust of the ground, and breathed into his nostrils the breath of life; and man became a living soul"* (KJV). There is no life in the dust. Moreover, after Adam and Eve sinned in the Garden of

Eden, God spoke to them concerning the death sentence they incurred due to sin. God reminded Adam and Eve of their lifeless origin—they were made out of dust from the ground—and sentences them to return to the ground from where they were taken. God told them, *"By the sweat of your brow you will eat your food until you return to the ground, since from it you were taken; for dust you are and to dust you will return"* (Genesis 3:19, NIV).

Returning to the dust means to die. Since then returning to dust is synonymous to dying, David comment indicates that his life circumstances can cause his death. Many times people's problems can kill them, and many times people's problems actually cause their death. Satan is capable of making you feel that death is the only solution to your dilemma. He makes you believe that death is the sovereign remedy for all your misfortune. Let me tell you, death is never the solution to your calamities. The solution is at the feet of the cross, at the feet of Jesus Christ, the Lord God, your creator. Do not even think about taking or ending your life because of the challenges you face. Live and look for a viable solution. Live and build stepping stones that will lead you to a successful life, a life that enjoys lasting success, and a life that ends in happiness and fulfillment.

> *Do not even think about taking or ending your life because of the challenges you face. Live and look for a viable solution.*

If your life is not successful, Satan has succeeded in his ability to deceive you. Do not accept the devil's deceit! God wants our lives to be filled with success, happiness, fulfillment, and contentment. These are goals we can achieve if we live in the mighty name of Jesus by the Spirit of the Lord of hosts. Just as God told the Old Testament prophet Zechariah that a great mountain can become a plain, the same can happen in your life. Any insurmountable challenge that plagues you can be reduced to a plain if you live by the Spirit of God. God lets Zechariah know that great changes can occur *"not by might, nor by power, but by my [God's] Spirit"* (Zechariah 4:6-7, KJV). So when King David attended to that critical point in his life, he did not seek to die. Rather, he cried out to God and made several requests to Him. Again in Psalm 119 we find the heartfelt words of David as he made requests to the Lord: *"[R]enew my life according to your word"* (v. 25, NIV), *"Now give me your instructions"* (v. 26, LB), *"Strengthen me according to your word"* (v. 28, NIV). Though David is in a desperate and destitute state, he knew to whom to turn for strength to endure the present situation, and he knew to whom to turn to get back on the right path that would lead him to a God-filled destiny that would change his misery to pleasure, his sadness to joy, and his waywardness to a directed path. What a wonderful prayer David prayed! Despite his circumstances, David fully understood that God could revive him and allow him to live by His Spirit. My friend, there is hope for your destiny. There is hope for your future. The difficulties of life are real—more real at some times than in others. But do not worry. Your destiny can still come to pass. You can still have a good future. You can still make it. You can still accomplish that long time dream.

Beloved, if you can just pray the prayer of David any time you feel that your soul is attached to the dust or when you feel that your soul is wrestling with the angel of death, call upon the Lord. He will strengthen you and give you life in abundance enough to continue the journey to your intended destiny. After all, Jesus Christ declares, *"My purpose is to give you life in all its fullness"* (John 10:10, NIV). Thus, death is never the remedy to your situation. Ask God to give you life and receive life in the Name of Jesus.

> *Any insurmountable challenge that plagues you can be reduced to a plain if you live by the Spirit of God.*

The Desire to Do Your Will—Not God's Will

Usually when you are discouraged and perplexed, the next move the devil gets you to make is to exercise your own will instead of the will of God. Whether you realize it or not, man cannot do anything without God's approval. The Bible declares, *"Many are the plans in a man's heart, but it is the Lord's purpose that prevails"* (Proverbs 19:21, NIV). It is important that we remember this scripture because, at times, circumstances may look with assurance as if the will of man prevails over the will of God. Be assured that such circumstances are temporary. God's will always prevails over Satan's if you obey and let Him lead you.

If you do not do the will of God, what do you think your destiny will be? Certainly, your destiny will not be what God intended for you. No matter how gifted or talented you are, you are no match for God. When you attempt to realize your destiny by using your own ideas, abilities, and actions without consulting the will of God, you are going to end up short every time. Your efforts without God equal nothing.

> *No matter how gifted or talented you are, you are no match for God.*

Even well-meaning people fall into the snares of Satan when they attempt to fulfill their own destiny. Satan will lead you to practice cheating, wickedness, idolatry, magic, occultism, sexual immorality, extortion, and the list goes on. Eventually you will regret your entanglement into sin if your intent is to reach your destiny by any of these means. For anything that comes from man's will and the devil's will is certain to destroy you in the end. Again, Jesus refers to Satan and his purpose as a thief, *"The thief comes only to steal and kill and destroy"* (John 10:10, NIV). So if you reject God and put your faith in the works of Satan, expect your destiny to be stolen, killed, and destroyed. No matter what occurs in your life, put your full trust in God. God can take your misfortunes and turn them into fortunes. The path to the destiny God wants you to have sometimes takes a route that you would not choose for yourself. You cannot always see what God sees, for the scripture reminds us how differently God thinks from the way we think, *"For my thoughts are not your thoughts, neither are your ways my ways. For as the heavens are higher than the earth, so are my ways higher than your ways, and my thoughts than your thoughts"* (Isaiah 55:8-9, KJV).

If you want to reach your destiny, enjoy it for life, and experience enjoyment and fulfillment at the end of your days; never do anything outside of the will of God. Configure God in every part of your life, and make sure He is the center of the important areas of your life. Therefore, confine your worship to God only; embrace the teachings of God as they relate to your profession and your actions in the workplace; let God be at the center of your marriage. You may ask the question: How do I know the will of God about these things? I will share this information with you in a later chapter.

> *God can take your misfortunes and turn them into fortunes.*

Spiritual Drowsiness

Another consequence of worry is the affliction of spiritual drowsiness. When you experience prolonged worry about your destiny, you have a tendency to doubt yourself; and the spirit of doubt can extend itself to cause you to doubt the existence, the power of God, and the ability of His Word. You will find yourself asking such questions as:

- Does God really exist?
- Does God care about me?
- Is God interested in me?
- Is God far from me?
- Is God slow or tardy?
- Is God really the Almighty?
- Is God wicked toward me?
- Does God listen to me and does He answer my prayers?

When such questions as these persist, eventually you will not trust God and His Word any more. In other words, you will lose your faith. God does not take pleasure in you when you no longer have faith in Him. The scripture addresses this issue in the book of Hebrews: *"And without faith it is impossible to please God, because anyone who comes to Him must believe that He exists and that He rewards those who earnestly seek Him"* (11:6, NIV). The Bible makes it very clear that if you do not believe and have faith that God exists, you cannot please Him. When you are dozing spiritually, you do not exercise the rituals that feed your faith. You do not fervently pray, fast, read the scriptures with the voraciousness that will make you spiritually strong and give you the faith and assurance that God will guide your destiny. Do not worry about your destiny to the point that you lose your faith in God. The Bible admonishes, *"Commit everything you do to the Lord. Trust Him to help you do it and He will"* (Psalm 37:5, LB). God can and will certainly bring your destiny to pass if you commit it into His hands. He is the author of your life and has the power and capacity to cause a successful, prosperous destiny to spring forth for you.

> *God does not take pleasure in you when you no longer have faith in Him.*

You Are Who You Are

The word of God came to the prophet Jeremiah saying, *"Before I formed you in the womb I knew you; before you were born I sanctified you; and I have established you . . ."* (Jeremiah 1:4). In this passage two words touch my heart— *"before"* and *"established."* The word "before" comparatively to what God declared to Jeremiah signifies *"in the beginning."* According to John 1:1-3, "in the beginning" means "since the foundation of the world or the universe" (Genesis 1:1 and Job 38:4) or before the world was created. The meaning of the word *"established"* makes me very joyful and confident about my destiny. To establish means to institute (as a law) permanently by enactment or agreement; it means to settle and to put beyond doubt. Wow!

In effect, the loving God told Jeremiah the decision to make him a prophet was made before he was conceived, and possibly the decision was made before God created the heavens and the earth. Walking back in time, it is an awesome thought to reconstruct all that had not taken place when God decided that Jeremiah would be a prophet for the nations. God decided that Jeremiah's destiny would be that of a prophet . . .

- Before Jeremiah's parents were born.
- Before Jeremiah's parents met one another.
- Before Jeremiah's parents married.
- Before Jeremiah's parents consummated their marriage.
- Before Jeremiah was conceived.
- Before Jeremiah was born.

The eternal God, the Great I Am, the Alpha and Omega established the destiny of Jeremiah—who he was, who he would be, and who he became. The success of Jeremiah's destiny played out according to God's plans because the prophet was obedient to God.

Likewise, God has made decisions about your destiny before you were conceived. Know that God's plan for your success has already been decided, but it is up to you to whether or not the fulfillment of God's plan comes to fruition. Nothing, nothing, nothing in the heavens, on the earth, underneath the seas; no power can separate you or stop you from reaching your destiny as long as you commit it into the hands of the creator, God Almighty. After going through the trials of Satan's attempt to destroy God's destiny for Job, Job declared with assurance, *"I know that you can do all things; no plan of yours can be thwarted (prevented)"* (Job 42:2, NIV).

> *Likewise, God has made decisions about your destiny before you were conceived.*

Understand this mystery. It was not when you were born in this world that you evolve into who you become and your destiny begins to unfold. God has determined who you will be before the foundation of the world was made. This is why your heart should not be troubled. Believe in God and He will be responsible for your destiny on earth.

How Can You Know Your Destiny?

First of all, I want you to understand that as a Christian, you don't need, and you are not even supposed to be consulting psychic and fortune tellers to know what your futuure holds. The Bible says, *"Let no one be found among you who practices divination or sorcery, interprets omens, engages in witchcraft"* (Deuteronomy 18:10 NIV). In fact, if you are in Christ and Christ is in you, you can easily know your destiny. You can know it by the Spirit of God by means of revelation. God has thousands of ways to reveal hidden things to His children at the appointed time. We see examples of such manifestations in the Old and New Testaments. I will mention a few means by which God revealed things to people as He directed their destiny. Whatever God did in the past, He can do it again. How did God reveal people's destiny to them? He communicated His messages through . . .

- Dreams
- Visions
- God's audible voice
- Conviction
- Circumstances
- Personal God-given talents or gifts

Dreams

A dream is a series of thoughts, images, or emotions occurring during sleep. Often times God used dreams to communicate to chosen ones. He used them to accomplish several purposes. The Bible tells us:

> *For God does speak—now one way, now another—though man may not perceive it. In a dream, in a vision of the night, when deep sleep falls on men as they slumber in their beds, He may speak in their ears and terrify them*

with warnings, to turn man from wrongdoing and keep him from pride, to preserve his soul from the pit, his life from perishing by the sword. (Job 33:14-18, NIV)

Joseph, the eleventh of Jacob's twelve sons, is one of many who received messages from God in a dream. God revealed Joseph's destiny to him in a dream, letting him know that the time would come when his father, mother, and eleven brothers would bow before him (Genesis 37:5-11). The previous reference to the scripture in Job lets us know that man does not always recognize messages when they are sent from the Lord. God can reveal your destiny to you in dreams as well. All you need to do is plug yourself into God, and sometimes you, also, can know the outcome of your destiny ahead of time.

When you have a dream, it is important to analyze it to make sure it is from God because all dreams do not come from Him. Dreams have three sources. A dream can come from God; it can be a message from the flesh, or it can be a message from Satan. You have to pray always and bring the message of your dream to the light of the Word of God to make sure the dream is from God. Your next task is to interpret the dream. If you have difficulty understanding the message, seek counseling from your spiritual leader to confirm whether or not the message is from God.

Visions

A vision is similar to a dream in that it is a vehicle through which God reveals supernatural insight or awareness. Dreams only occur during sleep, whereas visions occur when a person is awake. For example, Ezekiel, a priest and prophet of God, acknowledges that he was awake when God spoke to him in a vision and gave him the details of the message He wanted delivered to the Israelites. The children of Israel had become impudent, stiff-necked, hard-hearted, and rebellious toward God (Ezekiel chapters 1 and 2). As God gave Ezekiel instructions about how to present himself before the Israelites, He also revealed his destiny to him. Moreover, Daniel, a great prophet of God admits that he was awake when the Lord showed him a vision that put him in a trance and revealing to him what will happen to Israel and the world in the end (Daniel 10:7), and his destiny was foretold.

God's Audible Voice

Just as you hear a person talking to you, during the patriarchal, Old and New Testament period, and even now, God talked to selected people in an audible voice. God spoke to Moses in an audible voice telling him to go to Egypt to deliver the children of Israel from their oppression (Exodus 3:4). Christ spoke audibly to Saul (whose name was changed to Paul) to reprimand him about his persecution of the church and to instruct him about the destiny of his life (Act 9:1-6).

Conviction (Word of Knowledge)

Word of knowledge is a gift of the Holy Spirit; it is the revelation and comprehension of hidden and unknown information. The word of knowledge is also the transcendental revelation of the divine will and plan of God in human affairs. With the Holy Spirit comes a level of knowledge can be attributed only as a gift from the Divine. For instance, Elisha knew that his servant Gehazi lied to Naaman and extorted money and clothes from him (II Kings 5:20-27). Then there was the case in which Peter knew that Ananias and his wife, Sapphira lied to him and the Holy Ghost about the price of land they sold (Acts 5:1-8).

The gifts of wisdom and the word of knowledge work together. God can reveal your destiny to you by a strong persuasion or belief, which are convictions of the word of knowledge.

Circumstances

God can use circumstances, situations, or events in your life to navigate to your destiny. Before David knew that he would be crowned the king of Israel, an ordinary event occurred in his life that directed the path of his destiny. One day his father did an ordinary thing. His father sent him to the battlefield to see how his three sons who accompanied Saul to war were doing and to take food to them and their captain. When David arrived at the camp, he heard the ranting of the giant Goliath, and witnessed the fear of King Saul's army. David asked the rhetorical question, "[W]ho is this uncircumcised Philistine that he should defy the armies of the living God?" (I Samuel 17:26, KJV). Then he offered without fear to do battle with Goliath. To make a long story short, David confronted Goliath and killed him (I Samuel 17:40-51) according to the promise he made to King Saul and according to his trust in the Lord God of Israel. Stemming from a simple circumstance of an errand he made in obedience to his father, David gained a reputation, served in the palace of King Saul, and years later was ordained as the king of Israel according to the promise of God through the prophet Samuel (I Samuel 16:13-23).

God can use ordinary situations and events that occur in your life as a route to reveal and take you to your destiny. Keep your intelligence, knowledge, and understanding open as you navigate the situations of your life. For through these circumstances God may reveal to you the purpose for which you were born. I pray that the Lord will help you to recognize your primary destiny as He has set it in His master plan for your life as circumstances unfold.

Personal God-given Talents or Gifts

The wisdom of Solomon declares, *"A man's gift makes room for him and brings him before great men"* (Proverbs 18:16, RSV). Your natural endowment—a special, sometimes creative or artistic aptitude, general intelligence or skills—are indicators of who you are born to be and can direct you to your destiny. Seldom do people become something that they do not have the talent, gift, or ability to do. More on this subject will be discussed later.

Your Duty: Bring Your Destiny to Fruition

After you become aware of where your destiny will lead you, you have some responsibility to bring it to pass. It is one thing to know your destiny; it is something else to see that it is accomplished. Many people have known what their destiny was to be, but they never saw it realized. There are several steps you can take to make sure that your destiny comes to fruition.

Seek to know "how" your destiny can be fulfilled. Put yourself on the mission to search, study, learn what you need to do in order to fulfill your destiny. If you discover that your destiny is for you to become president, learn how to matriculate in the political arena. Study the local, state, and federal laws. Make the necessary business, social, and political connections. Learn the duties and functions of various government offices. Garner necessary constituencies. You also need to associate with godly people who can teach you and give you good advice. Groom yourself well for the task in every way necessary. In essence, you will perform these same or similar steps for whatever your destiny—minister, preacher, founder, doctor, lawyer, electrician, carpenter, hairstylist, teacher, mechanic, law enforcement officer, businessman/woman, and so forth. You have to look for how to become what you are meant to become after you have discovered.

Put what you know about yourself into action. You must take inventory of yourself. Be honest. What are your strengths? What are your talents? What are your skills? What are your interests? Once you have acknowledged your positive and negative points, you must go into action to strengthen your weaknesses. For example, if you are a procrastinator, develop a strategy for getting things done in a timely manner. If you are disorganized, develop organizational skills. If you are always late, work out strategies that get you to places ahead of time. If your communication skills are poor, get help. Read, study, take a class. If you are lazy, get busy! You have to work on your weaknesses because these can sabotage the success of your destiny. Action is the key. Start doing something about where you know God is leading you to. It may be difficult. People may be wondering about what you are doing, and say many things to discourage you. But be encouraged. Understand that every noticeable success always starts as a subject of mockery for people who know and don't know you; continues in criticism and humiliation. But surely, always ends in recognition and congratulations. Also, don't wait to have everything together before you start doing something about your destiny or purpose. At times you don't need everything to do something. Start doing something now about your destiny. There are books, audiotapes, websites, and classes that can give you the help you need for improving whatever problem (s) you have that can slow down or even prevent the fulfillment of your destiny and becoming the person God wants you to become.

Obey God in all that he expects you to do. Obedience to God is one of the conditions by which the Lord will definitely fulfill your destiny in life. When you obey God, you permit Him to accomplish His thoughts, plans, and divine purpose of your life. To obey God is to practice His ordinances—that is, you are to think, speak, act, and see according to His word. In other words, our lives must give God pleasure. And full obedience is what pleases God. A case in point is the command that God gave Saul to *"smi-*

ite Amalek, and utterly destroy all that they [the Amalekites] have, and spare them not; but slay both man and woman, infant and suckling, ox and sheep, camel and ass" (I Samuel 15:3, KJV). Saul was partially obedient to God in that he destroyed everyone except Agag, king of the Amalekites, and he destroyed everything that was vile and worthless, but he spared the best of all the animals. Later when Samuel confronted Saul because he did not carry out God's command to the letter, Saul gives the excuse, "But the people took of the spoil, sheep and oxen, the chief of the things which should have been utterly destroyed to sacrifice unto the Lord thy God in Gilgal" (I Samuel 15:21, KJV). To this comment, Samuel responded, *"Does the Lord delight in burnt offerings and sacrifices as much as in obeying the voice of the Lord? To obey is better than sacrifice, and to heed is better than the fat of rams. For rebellion is like the sin of divination, and arrogance like the evil of idolatry"* (I Sa-muel 15:22-23, NAS).

Beloved, what has God asked you to do in life? How does He expect you to make use of your talents, gifts, abilities? Precious one, always do what God wants you to do. Until you respond to God's command in its fullness, your happiness can never be complete in this world. For God did not send you in this world to do your will, but to do His will. Do not become stagnant trying to decide *"why"* God has ordained a particular mission for your life. Though there is nothing wrong with wanting to understand *why*, the more important concern is for you to be passionate about following the will of God for your life. Know that God wants you to be who He intended for you to be. If you really want to enjoy life and be satisfied on earth, let the purpose of God for you shine through in your life.

Be humble for God to elevate you. God loves to see a humble spirit in his children. In fact, a humble spirit is one of the virtues of Christianity. The Bible tells us, *"Humble yourselves, therefore, under God's mighty hand, that He may lift you up in due time"* (I Peter 5:6, NIV). To humble yourself before God is simply to respect Him and His authority. The mighty hand of God is the power of God, and anyone who is arrogant and proud has extended himself or herself beyond the protective shelter of God's hand. If you are not humble, you are outside of the operational circle of the presence and power of God.

There is a special bond God forms with people who are humble before Him and before mankind. Such was the case with Moses. The Bible describes Moses thusly: *"Now Moses was a very humble man, more humble than anyone else on the face of the earth"* (Numbers 12:3, NIV). God told Moses' brother and sister, Aaron and Miriam, in no uncertain terms about the special relationship He had with Moses. God explained to Aaron and Miriam that He talked with prophets by way of dreams and visions, but not so with Moses. Concerning Moses, God said, *"With him I speak face to face, clearly and not in riddles; he sees the form of the LORD"* (Numbers 12:8, NIV). So whoever is humble is under the mighty hand of God and can experience the full power of God in his life in a special measure.

Beloved, do not let the knowledge of your destiny or who you are seduce you to become arrogant and proud. If you humble yourself in the genuine spirit of meekness, God will elevate you to heights you did not imagine. *"God opposes the proud but gives grace to the humble"* (I Peter 5:5, NIV). An humble spirit should attend you at all times, everywhere, and in everything that you do before God and man. Humility is never weakness; it is a spiritual virtue that prompts God to be gracious to you as He assists you to accomplish your destiny. Finally, the Bible asks the rhetorical question*: "And what does the LORD require of you?"* (Amos 6:8, NIV). Following the question is the answer: *"To act justly and to love mercy and to walk humbly with your God"* (Amos 6:8, NIV).

The Power Of Success

Success is a good thing, but it can be dangerous to some who attain it. Do not become conceited in your success such that you begin to look down on others and think no one is like you. Satan will have you to think of God as the creation and not the Creator. He will make you forget that your source of being, your existence and your success have their origins in God. When your thinking becomes warped, then you will run into problems with God. The real, most attractive, and responsible success occurs in the person who recognizes that God the Almighty orchestrated the success and who maintains a humble Spirit as the success is enjoyed. Therefore, as you succeed, do not let the power of success turn you away from God or make you deviate from practices that you know to be right.

> *Success is a good thing, but it can be dangerous to some who attain it.*

- **Be faithful from beginning to end.** As you aspire to reach your destiny, always be loyal to God. I have studied the promises of God to men and women of the Old Testament and the New Testament, and I have found that God is exact in the accomplishment of His engagements and promises. The same is true today. God is always faithful to the promises He makes to everyone of His children from generations to generations. The Bible says, *"Not at all! Let God be true;__"* (Romans 3:4). Conversely, mankind has often been negligent in their engagements in life or destiny toward God and others once they achieve a degree of success. Your word has to be your bond. As the scripture says, *"Simply let your 'Yes' be 'Yes,' and your 'No,' 'No'; anything beyond this comes from the evil one"* (Matthew 5:37, NIV).

Beloved, how many promises have you broken? How many engagements have you accepted but did not fulfill? How many business or professional engagements have you not kept? How often have you failed to pray for a situation you said you would remember in prayer? How many times have you not supported a good work? As a general rule, God does not entrust you with great achievements and responsibilities if you cannot handle or manage the little ones He has given you. Often times the gifts and blessings of God are given on the basis of your fidelity to Him. If you are faithful in the small charges with which He entrusts in your care, God will release a great destiny to come forth on your behalf. The Lord will say to you, *"Well done, good and faithful servant! You have been faithful with a few things;* (Matthew 25:21, NIV).

Do you want to see the fulfillment of your destiny? Then be faithful to God even in the little tasks that He calls upon you to do now. Whatever the task, perform it well and with due diligence. Be faithful in your dealings with God and men.

- **Avoid sin in any form.** Sin is an offense against God and moral law. It is lawlessness and transgression of God's will, either by omitting to do what God's law requires or by doing what God's law forbids (I John 3:4). For your destiny to be accomplished with God's approval, and for you to have a destiny that is lasting and cannot be erased, avoid the practice of sin. I am not saying that you have to be perfect before your destiny can be fulfilled. It may happen that you make some mistakes along the journey to your purpose in life and to your ultimate destiny. God will deliver you and forgive you. But when you commit and practice sin knowingly, thinking God is good and merciful, and He will forgive you, you are building some serious problems for yourself that can hurt you and block your destiny as well.

Now you may say you know people who lived or are living a lawless and ungodly life, yet they are succeeding in life and moving toward what appears to be a destiny that is impressive and worthwhile. Right? Do not be blinded by what "seems" to look good, follow what happens as life continues for these people in their ungodly ways. Look at what happens at the end of their lives. The negative results can be staggering. They are not remembered for good. At the end of their lives they are good for nothing and hopeless. Sometimes they ridicule themselves by their own words and actions, and they die a shameful death.

Be aware that Satan will come at you any way that he can to tear down the spiritual fortress you are building to protect yourself from the evil one. Young Joseph was only seventeen when he received the revelation of his destiny to become the prime minister of Egypt. Joseph understood the urgency to stay away from sin, even flee from it if his destiny were to be fulfilled in the glorious manner God had in store for him. So when the wife of his master attempts to seduce Joseph, he verbally refused her advances saying, *"[H]ow . . . can I do this great wickedness and sin against God"* (Genesis 39:9, KJV)? But Potiphar's wife was relentless. The Bible says that she invited the handsome, young Joseph to go to bed with her day after day, but he continued to refuse her allurement. Finally, the master's wife lays a trap for Joseph and he literally ran out of his coat to get away from her (Genesis 39:10-12).

Because Joseph did not allow himself to become entrapped in sin, God fulfilled the young man's destiny in a way that was exceedingly successful (Genesis 41:39-46), lasting (Joseph lived to be 110 years old Genesis 50:22), and Joseph's long life came to a good end (Genesis 50:22-26).

Beloved, if you want your destiny to come to pass, last, and have a good end, fly away from sin in whatever way is necessary. Sometimes you may literally have to run away as did Joseph. Avoid the works of the sinful nature of the flesh—*"sexual immorality, impurity and debauchery, idolatry and witchcraft; hatred, discord, jealousy, fits of rage, selfish ambition, dissensions, factions, and envy, drunkenness, orgies, and the like"* (Galatians 5:19-21, NIV).

- **Practice prayer.** Prayer is communication with God in word or thought; it is speaking and listening to God, and an act of communion with God. In your prayers you can talk to God about everything that really matters—such as your fellowship with Him, getting to know Him better, and your destiny. Moreover, you can make request of God, such as, asking for His protection, asking for success in various endeavors, and asking for strength for a particular weakness you may have such as the need for self-control. I recommend that you develop a phenomenal prayer life. You may choose to get a good book on prayer, but especially study the prayer life of people in scripture such as David and Christ. A constant prayer life will help you to succeed in the challenges and tests that come your way as you move toward your ultimate destiny. Paul tells us, *"Devote yourselves to prayer, being watchful and thankful"* (Colossians 4:2, NIV).

- **Practice fasting.** Although fasting is not a commandment in scripture, it is expected of all believers in their Christian walk. In a conversation Jesus had with His disciples, He prefaced one of several points He made with the comment, *"[W]hen you fast"* (Matthew 6:16-17, NIV). Jesus did not say, "If you fast." Therefore, Jesus reveals through scripture that fasting is expected of believers. Fasting is a form of spiritual discipline, and it is a significant part of your Christian walk just as praying and studying the scriptures are integral parts of Christian living. Fasting is a means by which you can draw closer to God. Fasting is a means by which you can get God's attention. It is a powerful weapon of spiritual warfare that God has given His children. It is a means of crucifying the flesh, bringing the flesh into subjection by denying it for a time basic sustenance of food. A prolonged period of fasting will temporarily weaken the physical body, but it will strengthen the spiritual body. In scripture, people who fasted coupled it with prayer, therefore, we should follow the same example.

Why do you need to fast? The answer is found in Isaiah 58:6-7 and other scriptures. These are the proper reasons and various circumstances that bring you to the point of fasting.

- To bring justice
- To undo heavy burdens and break the yoke and bondage
- To free the oppressed and break the bands of wickedness
- To share food
- To provide shelter for the poor
- To clothe the naked
- To provide for one's family
- To mourn and repent (Joel 2:12)
- To receive God's instructions (Judges 20:26-28)
- To die to the flesh (Acts 10:30-48)
- To demonstrate humility and deliverance from bondages and the power of sin (Ezra 8:21-23; 10:1)
- To resist the devil's temptations (Matthew 4:1-2)
- To launch a religious mission (Acts 13:1-3; 14:20-23)
- For health and healing (II Samuel 12:15-23)
- For spiritual power to cast out demons (Matthew 17:14-21)
- To seek counsel (Judges 20:6-28)

The Passion Of Being Useful

CHAPTER FIVE

* Leave A Good Imprint In the World
* Be Useful to God
* Be Useful to Your Family
* Be Useful to the World
* The Inventors

The Passion Of Being Useful

CHAPTER FIVE

The Bible declares, *"You are the salt of the earth. But if the salt loses its saltiness, how can it be made salty again? It is no longer good for anything, except to be thrown out and trampled by men"* (Matthew 5:13).

Nothing in the world exists without a reason. Everything has importance. And most assuredly, people have significance in God's grand scheme. God innately equips people with natural and spiritual gifts so that each person has the opportunity to be profitable toward His plan in this world.

The Lord equips persons according to His sovereignty. Thus, whoever you are, you have a destiny or purpose in God's plan.

> *Nothing in the world exists without a reason.*

There is a reality of life that some people choose to ignore. Every person has the charge to live his or her life as God has prescribed, planned and expected. Therefore, everybody will have to give an account to God before His judgment seat concerning what he/she has done in this world, that is, how we have conducted our lives. For one who knows God and His mysteries, the earth is a mission field. Every individual has a precise mission to accomplish in this world which is why every person should seek to know the mission for which he or she is delegated. A person should not come on the earth, live a number of years, and die without leaving behind an impact, a mark, or a history which contains such hallmarks as testimonies of repentance or conversion, a steady walk with God, and acts of compassion, courage, determination, honesty, faithfulness, service, and a variety of other Christian virtues and expectations. I call this kind of history in a person's life clean and pure. If your history is not clean or pure, then you fall into the second category. The second history is the negative or bad history that I call dirty. It is the history of one's life that exposes ungodliness, a life that is strewn with such sinful acts as incredulity, wickedness, infidelity, cheating, idolatry, envy, selfishness, adultery, and a variety of other ungodly behaviors, characters and attitudes.

> *Therefore, everybody will have to give an account to God before His judgment seat concerning what he/she has done in this world, that is, how we have conducted our lives.*

Leave A Good Imprint In the World

God expects His people to live good lives, so that the good they have done in this life continues after their death. In His sermon on the mount, found in chapters 5, 6, and 7 of the book of Matthew, the Lord Jesus Christ gave His disciples powerful words of instruction which transformed them, and they in turn transformed the world. Jesus gave detailed instructions concerning issues of everyday living:

- The appropriate attitudes Christians should have (5:3-12)
- Being the salt of the earth (5:13)
- Being the light of the world (5:14-16)
- the consequence of breaking the commandments and teaching others to break the commandments as well (5:19)
- The reward of obeying and teaching the commandments to others (5:19)
- How to manage anger (5:22-24)
- How to handle your adversary (5:25-26)
- Marriage, forbidding to swear and how to make promises (5:31-37)
- Forgiving others (5:38-41)
- Giving to and sharing with others (5:42)

- Loving your enemies (5:43-47)
- Being perfect as our Father in heaven is perfect (5:48)
- How to go about doing good deeds (6:1-4)
- How to pray (6:5-15)
- How to fast (6:16-18)
- Laying up treasures in heaven (6:19-23)
- The benefits of serving God (6:24-32)
- Seeking the kingdom of God (6:33-34)
- Judging others (7:1-5)
- Preserving that which is holy (7:6)
- God's response to His children when they ask, seek, and knock (7:7-12)
- Which gate to enter that leads to eternal life (7:13-14)
- How to recognize false prophets (7:15-20)
- Who shall enter the kingdom of heaven (7:21-23)
- The earmarks of a wise man (7:24-25)
- The earmarks of a foolish man (7:26-27)

> *God expects His people to live good lives, so that the good they have done in this life continues after their death.*

Jesus told His disciples they were the salt of the earth. As the salt of the earth they were to "season" the earth with the teachings, wisdom and power of God. Moreover, they were to set the example in their own lives. As the salt of the earth, Christians are the salt of the church of God; they are the salt of their family (wife, husband, children, sister, brother, siblings), and they are the salt of their neighborhood, society and the world at-large. Each individual must take seriously the charge of being the salt of the world. This is our mission as children of God, and this is what makes us valuable to the cause of Christ. Conversely, if we lose our salty flavor we become useless, good for nothing. Just as the Lord Jesus Christ wanted the disciples to understand that they were useful to the world, you must serve the same purpose. You, also, must be useful three-fold:

- For God
- For your families
- For the world

> *Jesus told His disciples they were the salt of the earth. As the salt of the earth they were to "season" the earth with the teachings and wisdom of God.*

Be Useful to God.

You need to be useful to God in the places you give Him in your life, in your service for Him, and in your worship to Him. Foremost, you are profitable to God when you serve Him with your life at home, your local church, your neighborhood, and on your job. So many people think that one has to be a minister, evangelist, prophet, or pastor in order to be useful to God. This is a false assumption. There are numerous ways you can be of service to God—through personal evangelism, through maintaining God's house, through sponsorship of mission and evangelistic endeavors

, and through much more. However, if you know God has called you to serve full time, do not give the Lord excuses. There is no greater calling than to be an ambassador, minister, or priest of God.

> *Foremost, you are profitable to God when you serve Him.*

Useful Men and Women in the Bible

Noah

Noah was useful to God because he served Him faithfully and because he lived an exemplary life among the people of his time when *"the wickedness of man was great [on] the earth, and . . . every imagination of the thoughts of [man's] heart was only evil continually"* (Genesis 6:5). Noah preached to them the message of God and exhorted them to turn away from their wicked ways. According to God's instructions, Noah invested his life in building an ark which would eventually become the ark of safety for those who lived in a sinful and dying world but who chose to obey God's commands rather than follow the wickedness of man (Genesis chapters 6, 7, 8, and 9).

Abraham

Abraham was one of the great patriarchs who lived his life in a way that was useful to God. He accepted God's call for him to leave his father's house and go into a far country that was unfamiliar to him. God's plan was to use Abraham to become the father of a great nation. Because of Abraham's great faith in God, he answered the call to go into a strange land where he would dwell with his immediate family. As a result of Abraham's obedience, God fulfilled all the promises He made to His servant. Thus, God made of Abraham a great nation; He made Abraham a great name, and He blessed Abraham abundantly (Genesis 12:1-9 and Hebrews 11:8-19).

Moses

Moses was one of the great leaders of the Israelites who consecrated his life to serve God. Through his obedience to God, Moses led the children of Israel out of Egypt with mighty signs, wonders, and miracles. He served as a shepherd, counselor, judge, and spiritual leader to the Israelites as they wandered through the desert forty years, serving as an able leader through all kinds of troubles, challenges, wars, rebellions, persecutions, and calamities until his death at 120 years old (Deuteronomy 34:1-12; Hebrews 11:23-30).

Joshua

The successor to Moses, Joshua, used his life for God. After serving as Moses' understudy, he became the leader of the Israelites following Moses' death. He was obedient to God's commands as was Moses. Consequently, Joshua completed the mission that Moses had begun. He led the children of Israel to conquer the promised land; he won battles and possessed the land from thirty-one kings, and he distributed the conquered territories among the twelve tribes of Israel according to the instructions of God (Deuteronomy 34:7-12; Joshua 12:24 and chapters 13-21).

Deborah, Gideon, Jephthah, Samson, Samuel, Ezra, Nehemiah, Ruth, and Esther

The Bible is replete with examples of people, both men and women who used their lives in special ways to accomplish God's bidding.

- **Deborah**, prophetess and judge of Israel, accompanied Barak into battle against Jabin, the king of Canaan, to encourage him to obey God's command (Judges chapters 4 and 5).
- **Gideon** listened to God's instructions for him to reduce his army from 32,000 to 300 men before going into battle against the Midianites, Amalakites, and enemies of the east, facing a foe so large that the warriors could not be numbered. Because Gideon was obedient to all of God's instructions, his army of 300 men defeated their foes handily (Judges chapters 6-9).
- **Jephthah**, the son of a harlot who was cast out of his father's house by his brothers, because Jephthah did not have the same mother as they, used his life for God. He became a mighty man of valor and joined forces with the elders of Gilead to defeat the Ammonites who fought against the children of Israel (Judges chapters 11 and 12).
- **Samson** used his life for God for a special purpose. God made special provisions surrounding

the birth of Samson. He was groomed to deliver the children of Israel out of the hands of the Philistines (Judges chapters 13-16).

- **Hannah's** decision to dedicate her son, Samuel, to God set the wheels in motion for his life to be special. Samuel was taught from childhood under the tutelage of Eli, the priest. He was a prophet and ultimately became the last judge of Israel before Israel began to be ruled by kings. He traveled an annual circuit traveling from Ramah to Bethel, Gilgal, and Mizpeh before returning to Ramah. As Samuel traveled from place to place his task was several-fold—judging the people, warning the children of Israel against worshipping idols, and using his influence to keep the tribes faithful to God (I Samuel chapters 1-7).
- **Ezra** used his life to restore God's people to Him when he left the captivity of Babylon, a member of the second migration of people who went to Jerusalem to restore the temple and to bring God's people back to the teachings of the law (Ezra chapters 7-10).
- **Nehemiah** used his life to rebuild the wall of Jerusalem after portions of it had been destroyed and left to lay in ruin. Upon going to Jerusalem Nehemiah added the task of strengthening the children of God (Nehemiah chapters 1-7).
- **Ruth's** conversion from the idolatrous worship of the Moabite god to Judaism brought about a change in her life that made her useful to God.

Ruth's devotion to her mother-in-law, Naomi, and Naomi's God positioned her to be used by God in a special way. After her husband's death, she married a kinsman, Boaz. Her marriage to Boaz produced a son, Obed. Obed became the father of Jesse, and Jesse became the father of David, the great warrior and king of Israel (Ruth chapters 1-4).

- **Esther** is another outstanding woman in the Bible and the second woman for whom one of the Old Testament books is named. She used her life to save the Jews from complete annihilation at the hands of Haman, an arrogant, egotistical advisor to the king of Shushan (Esther chapters 1-10).

Paul

Of the people featured in this list of examples of persons whose lives have been used for God, Paul is the only one named whose life is played out in the New Testament. Paul has been chosen because he represents the best of what a Christian will do to use his life for God. Before Paul understood the truth of God, he persecuted the church. However, after his conversion, he lived a phenomenal life in which he honored God. Let Paul tell you himself about his life as one who was useful to God. He gives a personal testimony in II Corinthians 11:23-28, NIV as he takes a moment to boast about his commitment to the work of the Lord:

"I have worked much harder [than any other Hebrew, Israelite, or person who is of the seed of Abraham—all des-

criptions of Paul], [I have] been in prison more frequently, been flogged more severely, and been exposed to death again and again. Five times I received from the Jews the forty lashes minus one. Three times I was beaten with rods, once I was stoned, three times I was shipwrecked, I spent a night and a day in the open sea, I have been constantly on the move. I have been in danger from rivers, in danger from bandits, in danger from my own countrymen, in danger from Gentiles; in danger in the city, in danger in the country, in danger at sea; and in danger from false brothers. I have labored and toiled and have often gone without sleep; I have known hunger and thirst and have often gone without food; I have been cold and naked. Besides everything else, I face daily the pressure of my concern for all the churches".

What a testimony! In addition, during all of these trials and tribulations Paul preached the gospel, bringing the light of God's Word to many cities and countries. Also, he wrote fourteen epistles out of the twenty-one letters penned in the New Testament. When we look at the life of Paul, we are forced to ask ourselves, what sacrifices are we making to the cause of Christ? What work are you engaged in at your local church? What are you doing about the lost souls around you? What are you doing about gospel missions? What are you doing with your life to make it useful in a world whose people stumble in spiritual darkness? Think about this seriously.

Be Useful to Your Family

God has a special purpose for every family. I discovered in

the Bible that God has precise thoughts, purposes, and plans for every family on earth. Though there are some expectations of families that are common to all families of God, there are some features of God's plans that are not the same from family to family. For example, God expects all families that espouse His teaching to love Him, to keep His commandments, and to demonstrate the fruit of the Spirit—*love, joy, peace, long-suffering, gentleness, goodness, faith, meekness, and temperance* (Galatians 5:22). On the other hand, there are families for whom God has a specific purpose.

> *God has precise thoughts, purposes, and plans for every family on earth.*

For example, in the book of Genesis we find the first family—Adam, Eve, and their offspring. God gave Adam and Eve two specific charges as a family. First, they were instructed to "[b]e *fruitful and multiply, and replenish the earth*" (Genesis 1:28 KJV). Second, they were instructed to "*subdue [the earth] and have dominion over the fish of the sea, and over the fowl of the air, and over every living thing that move[s] upon the face of the earth*" (Genesis 1:28, KJV).

When God decided to destroy the world, He needed a family to populate the world again after its destruction. Noah and his family are the ones chosen for this task. Apparently God was pleased with Noah's role as the patriarch of his family. The Bible says of this man, "*But Noah found grace in the eyes of the Lord*" (Genesis 6:8, KJV).

God had a purpose for the family of Abraham since the

foundation of the world. He planned for the birth of the Messiah (Jesus Christ) who would save the world to come through the lineage of Abraham. The New Testament opens with the genealogy of Christ showing His connection to the family of Abraham: *"A record of the genealogy of Jesus Christ the son of David, the son of Abraham"* (Matthew 1:1).

Later in the book of Genesis we are introduced to the family of Jacob (whose name was changed to Israel). All of Jacob's family members are interesting in the way that God chooses to use them. However, of particular importance is the eleventh one of the sons, Joseph. Joseph was purposed in God's plan to fulfill a special mission—to deliver his father's household, the family of Jacob from the destruction and death of a famine that consumed the whole earth (Genesis 41:54-57). His mission also was to serve as a prophet, speaking the words of God so that the Lord God of heaven would be glorified.

> *Joseph was purposed in God's plan to fulfill a special mission—to deliver his father's household, the family of Jacob from the destruction and death of a famine that consumed the whole earth.*

In the book of Exodus we are introduced to the family of Levi, a descendant from one of the sons of Jacob and Joseph's brother. God had several special missions for the Levite family—Amram (Moses' father), Jochebed (Moses' mother), Miriam and Aaron (Moses' sister and brother) and Moses. Though not much is said about Amram in the scriptures, the strength of his spiritual leadership is noted in the faith, strength, and courage of his family. Jochebed used her life to care for and nurture her own son, though she cannot claim him because he was adopted by the Pharaoh's daughter. Despite her enslavement, she secretly nurtured Moses in the tradition of the Jews, so that the thinking, beliefs, and practices of the Jews are innately his thought. A word of note is that Moses did not bow down to any idols, even though idolatry was a strong practice in Egypt. This speaks for the diligent teaching of his mother. Miriam's purpose was to watch her baby brother to see what happened to him when Jochebed placed her three month old son in a basket and set the basket to sail on the Nile River. When the Pharaoh's daughter took the baby for her own, it was Miriam who directed Moses' adoptive mother to Jochebed to become the baby's nurse. Later, Miriam became a prophetess (Exodus 15:20). Aaron's role began as Moses' personal spokesman because Moses did not have the confidence to speak before Pharaoh (Exodus 4:10-16). Aaron's highest call to purpose was to be ordained as High Priest (Exodus 28:1) of Israel, whose job was to represent the people before God, to offer the various sacrifices for sin and worship, and to teach the people the laws of God. Finally, Moses' purpose was to lead the children of Israel out of Egypt and to lead them to the promised land.

> *Though not much is said about Amram in the scriptures, the strength of his spiritual leadership is noted in the faith, strength, and courage of his family.*

Understand that you and your family have a purpose to fulfill. There is a reason for the people who make up the members of your family have been brought together. Together, as a family, you should seek to discover God's purpose for you in His plan of salvation.

> *Understand that you and your family have a purpose to fulfill.*

Moreover, how profitable are you to God in your individual walk with Him? Is God glorified in the life you live? Is the world better because you live in it? If you are born again, what are you doing to help others to be born again? If you are rich, what are you doing to relieve the discomfort and poverty of others? What are you doing to contribute to the spiritual welfare and growth of your family and others whom you influence? In other words, are you the salt of the earth, or has your salt lost its flavor?

Be Useful to the World.

God expects you to be useful wherever you find yourself in the world. As we grow, we are expected to extend the reaches of our influence. First, we have to be useful to God within ourselves, that is, using our natural and spiritual gifts, skills, and know-how to God's glory. Then we extend ourselves to our family, doing those things which are physically and spiritually profitable for them. From here, we begin to focus on the community, again extending our reaches further as we contribute to the good and well-being of our neighbors, co-workers, and acquaintances. Some persons will be given the opportunity to reach still further such that they find themselves positioned to influence a nation and the international world toward the righteousness of God and their well-being.

> *God expects you to be useful wherever you find yourself in the world. As we grow, we are expected to extend the reaches of our influence.*

For example, Moses, who was groomed as a prince of Egypt, found himself thrust into a situation in which he had to defend the cause of the Jewish nation:

> *One day, after Moses had grown up, he went out to where his own people were and watched them at their hard labor. He saw an Egyptian beating a Hebrew, one of his own people. Glancing this way and that and seeing no one, he killed the Egyptian and hid him in the sand. The next day he went out and saw two Hebrews fighting. He asked the one in the wrong, "Why are you hitting your fellow Hebrew?"* (Exodus 2:11-13, NIV).

Because of the special circumstances of Moses' birth and upbringing, he did not live his life openly practicing his Jewish heritage. A passion for his people had secretly been instilled in him by his mother. So one day when he sees an Egyptian beating a Hebrew, he saved his fellow countryman and killed the Egyptian. The next day Moses was moved to action again when he witnessed two Hebrews fighting. Ultimately, these two incidents impacted Moses' life and caused him to flee from home, a place he stayed away from for forty years. During the interim between leaving and returning home, Moses was groomed to become the leader of a nation. God used him to fulfill a purpose—to deliver the children of Israel from Egyptian slavery.

Is your life moving in a direction that will allow you to extend your reaches far beyond your immediate surroundings? Pay attention to what the Lord is doing in your life. Are you amenable to growing in ways that will make you fit so that God can use you to do greater things for Him? Think about it.

> *Pay attention to what the Lord is doing in your life. Are you amenable to growing in ways that will make you fit so that God can use you to do greater things for Him? Think about it.*

Who would have dreamed that a shepherd boy would rise to become king of Israel? A look back at David's life will reveal that he was taking steps all along to be useful to God. As a young boy, he developed the attributes necessary to be a great leader of people through what he learned while tending to sheep. His faith in God gave him the courage to do the unthinkable. When King Saul of Israel was fearful of the giant, Goliath, David told the king a story that convinced him to allow David to confront this great enemy of Israel:

> *"Your servant has been keeping his father's sheep. When a lion and a bear came and carried off a sheep from the flock*

I went after it, struck it and rescued the sheep from its mouth. When it turned on me, I seized it by its hair, struck it and killed it. Your servant has killed both the lion and the bear; this uncircumcised Philistine will be like one of them, because he has defied the armies of the living God. The LORD who delivered me from the paw of the lion and the paw of the bear will deliver me from the hand of this Philistine" (I Samuel 17:34-37, NIV).

Because David was useful to God and God could depend on him, he followed Saul, becoming the second king of Israel. His passion for doing the will of God and fulfilling God's purposes earned David one of the finest accolades God has ever given to one of His servants. Speaking about David, God said, *"I have found David son of Jesse a man after my own heart; he will do everything I want him to do"* (Acts 13:22, NIV).

> *His passion for doing the will of God and fulfilling God's purposes earned David one of the finest accolades God has ever given to one of His servants.*

Esther is another example of a follower of God extending the reach of God's purpose beyond self, family, and neighbors. When she is confronted with the opportunity to save the Jewish people from complete annihilation, she accepted the challenge. She remarked, *"For how can I bear to see disaster fall on my people? How can I bear to see the destruction of my family?"* (Esther 8:6).

THE PASSION OF BEING USEFUL

The Inventors

I want to take a point of privilege to shine the light on a group of people who have made outstanding contributions to the world because of their marvelous inventions. Though the inventions were not made from the perspective of them serving a spiritual cause, they do in large measure. If fact, I urge you to use your imagination to think of ways in which the inventions I am about to cite have an impact on spiritual matters.

> *Though the inventions were not made from the perspective of them serving a spiritual cause, they do in large measure.*

There have been some good inventions of the ages. I think about these inventions and how useful they are to humanity. The accessibility of being able to read and write today started with those who invented the alphabet over the centuries and *Johannes Gutenberg,* the German inventor of the movable-type printing press. It should be noted that the first book the printing press produced was a Latin Bible printed in 1455.

Mike Faraday, an English physicist and chemist, is credited with investigating, discovering, and understanding the laws of the magnetic field and electric currents. His inventions of electromagnetic rotary devices formed the foundation of electric motor technology, and it was largely due to his efforts that electricity became viable for use in technology.

I cannot help but think of *Thomas Edison's* invention of the electric light bulb when I turn on a light, and I think of *Philippe Lebon* when I see a gas light. *Robert Stephenson* created locomotives, so think about him when you ride a train. Another mode of transportation was invented by two brothers, *Wilbur and Orville Wright* and other pioneers of aircraft inventions such as another set of brothers, *Joseph and Jacques Mongolfier*, Frenchmen who invented the hot-air balloon, an important step in the development of aeronautics. *Otto Lilienthal*, a German civil engineer whose fundamental research on birds and airfoils led him to found the science of wing aerodynamics and lay the foundations for concepts still employed today. Both his research and his successful flights between 1891 and 1896 inspired the *Wright brothers*. He influenced their research that resulted in the invention of the powered, controllable, and heavier than air aircraft beginning in 1896 until their ultimate success in 1903. *Octave Chanute*, a French-born aviator pioneer, assisted the *Wright brothers* and studied the dynamics of hang-gliding, among other aviator concerns. And *Hermon L. Grimes*, another aviator pioneer, invented the first automatic folding wing airplane, an invention that *President Franklin D. Roosevelt* used during World War II. For the invention of the automobile, we have to thank such persons as *Karl Benz, Henry Ford,* and others.

Throughout history the world has profited from these contributions and others that men and women have made as they realized their dreams and aspirations. Though all of the aforementioned inventors are dead, their work lives on. What a legacy!

The same holds true for followers of God. We should look forward to leaving a spiritual legacy that lives long after we are gone. Following Jesus' resurrection and before He ascended into heaven, He appeared to His disciples and told them, *"Peace be with you! As the Lord has sent me, I am sending you"* (John 20:21, NIV). If the Lord is sending us into the world as the Father sent Him, then we have to be spiritually profitable to the world as Christ was spiritually profitable to the world. Do good to all people. As the Bible instructs, *"Do not withhold good from those who deserve it, when it is in your power to act"* (Proverbs 3:27, NIV).

> *If the Lord is sending us into the world as the Father sent Him, then we have to be spiritually profitable to the world as Christ was spiritually profitable to the world. Do good to all people.*

Precious one, live your life in a way that you are useful to God, your family, your community, and the world. The Lord Jesus Christ says, *"Behold I am coming soon! My reward is with me, and I will give to everyone according to what he has done"* (Revelation 22:12, NIV). Be useful! Be the salt of the earth! Leave your positive imprint on the world! Do it even now!

> *Precious one, live your life in a way that you are useful to God, your family, your community, and the world.*

Through or With Somebody

CHAPTER SIX

* *Relations With Others Can Take You Where You Cannot Go By Yourself*
* *Beware the Traps of the devil*

Through or With Somebody

CHAPTER SIX

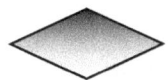

First of all, let me say this: No one can become somebody without somebody, and no one can become somebody without God. To build a life that is successful, you need others sometime, somewhere, somehow by the sovereign will of God. The people you need in your life come from a plethora of persons who naturally flow through your life — some to stay, others as transients. There are many persons who touch your life such as parents, grandparents, siblings, spouse, extended relatives, teachers, friends, bosses, co-workers, husband or wife, sometimes even strangers. They make contributions to your life in various ways, sometimes molding and shaping you, sometimes sharing words of wisdom, sometimes providing guidance—all in the broad scheme of shaping you into the person God intends for you to be. Without knowing so, these people are dispatched to assist God into shaping your life for His service.

When we give our lives over to God, He helps men, women and children to become who He created them to be and to do what will fulfill His purpose in them. In His sovereign will, God uses others on earth to accomplish His purpose and plan in our lives. Let's go to the scriptures to confirm this statement.

- God used Laban to bless Jacob (Genesis chapters 29 and 30).
- God used the daughter of Pharaoh to save the life of baby Moses and to groom him for the destiny that was to be his years later (Exodus 2:1-25).
- God used David to deliver Israel from the hand of Goliath and the Philistines (I Samuel 17:1-58).
- God used Esther to deliver the children of Israel from death in Babylonia (Esther chapters 3-5).
- God used the Lord Jesus Christ to save humanity (John 3:16).

No one can become somebody without somebody, and no one can become somebody without God.

There are many examples in the Bible which show that

THROUGH OR WITH SOMEBODY

God uses people on earth to accomplish His bidding. Irrespective of how much of a genius you might be, how talented, powerful, and anointed you may be, you cannot build a successful life all by yourself. You need other persons from which to learn a great deal. You need someone to teach you some of the basic truths of life. Usually this is the responsibility of parents and teachers. But beyond their teaching, you need others to instruct you in various areas in your life. God did not design man to be an island. He made us interdependent on one another. Just think, even though Christ was divine, He still depended on others to help Him to fulfill His purpose and to achieve the success He experienced on earth. For example:

- God used Joseph and Mary to serve as Christ's earthly parents (Matthew 1:18-24).
- God used John the Baptist to baptize Jesus (Matthew 3:13-17).
- God used a great many people—the lame man (Mark 2:1-12), the blind man (Mark 8:22-26), the woman at the well (John 4:5-42), the boy with the five loaves of bread and two fish (Mark 6:35-44), Jairus' daughter (Mark 5:21-43), Peter's mother-in-law (Matthew 8:14-15), among others—to demonstrate the power of God and to glorify Him.
- God used the apostles to spread the message of the Gospel throughout the world (Acts 8:4).
- God used Peter and Paul in special ways to demonstrate the power of God (Acts 19:11-12 and Acts 5:12-15).
- God used Joseph of Arimathea to supply a tomb for Christ when the Savior died (Luke 23:50-56).

- God used Ananias to assist in the conversion of Saul (named later changed to Paul), baptize, and comfort him following Saul's miraculous encounter with Jesus on the road to Damascus (Acts 9:1-22).
- God used Christ's disciples to spread the news of His resurrection (Luke 24:33-35).

> *God did not design man to be an island. He made us interdependent on one another.*

Relations With Others Can take You Where You Cannot Go by Yourself.

Developing good relationships with people by the direction of the Holy Spirit and according to the will of God is one habit you should practice as you go through life. The relationships we develop with the right people transport us along the highway of life to places we would not necessarily get to on our own. We need an arsenal of people to assist us in various areas of our lives that will help us to be successful. First and foremost, we need people in our lives who love the Lord and walk by His Word to be closely associated with us for spiritual support. Following these people, we need persons in our lives who will assist us spiritually, physically, medically, intellectually, materially and financially, among other areas of need. The right information that this support group of people offer, or the lack thereof, can change the course of your life for good or bad.

We have no way of knowing how or when someone will

THROUGH OR WITH SOMEBODY

have an impact on our lives that can be a turning point. This is one reason it is good to be kind to everyone and to treat people with respect. The Bible says, *"So in everything, do to others what you would have them do to you, for this sums up the Law and the Prophets"* (Matthew 7:12). You can never tell whom God will use to assist you on your journey to achieve success in your life.

> *We have no way of knowing how or when someone will have an impact on our lives that can be a turning point. This is one reason it is good to be kind to everyone and to treat people with respect.*

Despite how powerful and influential people may be, do not make the mistake of putting more of your trust in relationships with people than you do in God. Yes, God will use people to bless your life in a number of ways, but do not let them supersede the place of God in your trust and in your life. You do not want to hinder your life by misdirecting your loyalty. The wisdom of David from the Psalms tells us, *"It is better to take refuge in the Lord than to trust in man"* (Psalm 118:8, NIV).

Certainly, God will use people to bless you and bring your destiny to fulfillment, but do not put your trust in people and forget the God who causes them to be a blessing to you. The Bible declares, *"Do not put your trust in princes, in mortal men, who cannot save"* (Psalm 146:3).

> *Certainly, God will use people to bless you.*

Beware the Traps of the devil

Beware of the traps of the devil when praying for relationships, people, and things God can use to bring your destiny to fruition. Satan will sometimes intervene and send you somebody or something that is a FAKE to alter your path to prevent you from reaching the desired destination. For Satan is the great deceiver. The apostle Paul warns us that not only will Satan deceive us, but there are times when he will send his emissaries to do the same. Paul calls them *"deceitful workmen."* He warns the Christians at Corinth: *"And I will keep on doing what I am doing in order to cut the ground from under those who want an opportunity to be considered equal with us in the things they boast about. For such men are false apostles, deceitful workmen, masquerading as apostles of Christ. And no wonder, for Satan himself masquerades as an angel of light. It is not surprising, then, if his servants masquerade as servants of righteousness"* (II Corinthians 11:12-15). Therefore, you must be circumspect. The Lord Jesus Christ says, *"I am sending you out like sheep among wolves. Therefore, be as shrewd as snakes and as innocent as doves"* (Matthew 10:16, NIV).

> *Beware of the traps of the devil when praying for relationships, people, and things God can use to bring your destiny to fruition.*

Remember, God will use people and allow opportunities to bring your destiny to fulfillment. But in so doing, you have to be sure that these come from God and not the great deceiver, Satan.

The Great Instruction

CHAPTER SEVEN

* *Calculate to Choose the One and Only true God*
* *Calculate to Choose the Right Career*
* *Calculate to Choose the Right Spouse*
* *What It Takes to be Successful*
* *Jesus the Rock*
* *Endurance*
* *Pass It On*

The Great Instruction

CHAPTER SEVEN

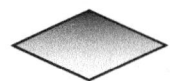

One day when the Lord Jesus Christ was having dinner at the house of a Pharisee, He spoke these words, *"For which of you, intending to build a tower, does not first sit down and estimate the cost, to see whether he has enough to complete it? Otherwise, when he has laid a foundation and is not able to finish, all who see it will begin to ridicule him, saying, 'This fellow began to build and was not able to finish"* (Luke 14:28-30, NRSV).

Beloved, I have said throughout this discourse that life is to be built. To give you a very clear understanding of what it means to build a life that is spiritually and physically successful, a life that enjoys lasting success, and a life that ends well, I am going to follow the instructions Jesus gave His disciples and others who listened to Him. I call Jesus' message THE GREAT INSTRUCTION because this is a message that is needed in every area of a person's life. Most of the things which work together to build a successful life are founded on Jesus' words.

> *Life is to be built.*

Christ used the illustration of building a tower to instruct His listeners, but I am using the illustration of building a house. Life is like a house that a builder constructs, and the calculations the construction worker uses determines whether the builder comes to a happy, successful outcome or whether the outcome is a miserable failure.

Sightseeing and looking at houses is for some people a great American pastime. As we pay particular attention to houses, especially when we are house-hunting, we are impressed by the architecture of some houses—the design, the craftsmanship, the beauty of the structure. Conversely, when we see houses we do not like, we comment on what we see as the negatives regarding the house—its poor design, its lack of craftsmanship, and its lack of beauty.

We view people's lives in much the same manner in which we assess houses. When we see the life of a person who is allowing God to have full reign of his life, we admire the spiritual architectural beauty of that life—God's design and craftsmanship of it. On the other hand, when we see the life of a person who is allowing Satan to have the controlling interest in the architectural design of that life, we make all kinds of negative comments concerning what is wrong with it. When a life is successful, people praise it. When a life is a failure, men mock it and ridicule it unabashedly. Therefore, I challenge you to build your life by using spiritual and practical calculations that will guarantee your success. And by so doing, you can bring glory and honor to God in your life.

> *I challenge you to build your life by using spiritual and practical calculations that will guarantee your success.*

To review Christ's message in Luke 14:28-30 is to realize that estimating the cost of building calls for some calculations. Once we have accessed the cost of building, then we know whether or not we have the funds to begin and finish successfully what we want to construct. I find Christ's use of the "building/construction" metaphor interesting because this metaphor appears several times in the Bible. In speaking to the church at Corinth, Paul tells the members of the church that they are God's *"building"* (I Corinthians 3:9, KJV). He further tells them, *"According to the grace of God which is given unto me, as a wise master builder, I have laid the foundation [regarding the teachings of Christ]"* (I Corinthians 3:10, KJV). This metaphor of calculating appears again in scripture: *"By wisdom the Lord laid the earth's foundations, by understanding he set the heavens in place"* (Proverbs 3:19, NIV). God Himself calculated the measurements of heaven and earth when He made the universe. In a very poignant passage of scripture when God talks to Job, calculations entered the equation when He questioned Job:

> *"Then the Lord answered Job out of the storm. He said, . . . "Brace yourself like a man; I will question you, and you shall answer me. Where were you when I laid the earth's foundation? Tell me, if you understand. Who marked off its dimensions? Surely you know. Who stretched a measuring line across it? On what were its footings set, or who laid its cornerstone . . . Have you journeyed to the springs of the sea, or walked in the recesses of the deep? . . . Have you comprehended the vast expanses of the earth?"* (Job 38: 1, 3-6, 16, 18, NIV).

> *God Himself calculated the measurements of heaven and earth when He made the universe.*

Thus, counting up the cost is an instruction that we should not fail to do spiritually nor otherwise. Am I saying we should ignore faith? Absolutely not! I am saying make your calculations in connection with your faith. There are people who make calculations and ignore having faith. Conversely, there are people who have faith who fail to do the calculations. Both of these ways of living your life will prove to be faulty. You must strike a balance so that you will have a clear direction as you are guided by the Holy Spirit.

> *You must strike a balance so that you will have a clear direction as you are guided by the Holy Spirit.*

Calculate to Choose the One and Only true God

Some people are suffering through living an unsuccessful life because they have not calculated upon choosing the right God to rule and guide their lives. Some have given themselves over to various religious orders, sects, and secret societies. Others have allowed themselves to fall prey to demons and evils spirits. Others have become their own God through seeking to please themselves and through thinking of themselves more highly than they should. In all of these cases, persons espousing these faulty paths that do not please God will find that their lives will not end well if they do not change direction and travel a path that is pleasing to God. Also, the decision they make can affect the family for future generations.

> *Also, the decision they make can affect the family for future generations.*

It is amazing the number of religious practices people engage themselves as they seek to build a life that is successful. They practice witchcraft, magic, voodoo, enchantments, divination, and multiple other rituals designed to guide their lives. For a while life will sail along just fine, but rest assured that in the long run, the demons will turn on the people who are practitioners of the occult. These demons will start to make people's lives miserable through manifestations of physical and mental illnesses, accidents, suicides, and deaths. In addition, money, material possessions, popularity and fame will dwindle and sometimes disappear altogether.

You have the obligation to investigate any church, organization, association, or society that professes to be a religious group. There are several questions that come to mind that should be answered to determine whether or not the worship group is sanctioned by God.

- Do they ignore the commandments of God?
- Do they condemn the Word of God?
- Do they change or alter the Word of God?
- Do they promote abominations such as lying (Proverbs 12:22), homosexuality (Leviticus 18:22 and Leviticus 20:13), stealing, murder, adultery, false swearing, and following other gods (Jeremiah 7:9-10), among other abominations mentioned and identified in the scriptures as such.
- Do they provoke and encourage people to sin?
- Do they destroy the marriage, careers, and lives of people?
- Do they endanger the lives of people, and/or do they kill people and their children?
- Do they practice dominating specific places or territories?
- Do they resist men of God?
- Do they afflict people in some way?
- Do they possess people or control the lives of people?

If you answer "yes" to one or more of these questions, you are attending the wrong place of worship, and you are not worshipping and serving the only true God. However, if your response is "no," it is more than likely that you are in a fellowship that meets God's approval. God the creator, the almighty is the one God who can help you build the life you seek that is successful, lasting, and that ends well. When we are obedient to the Lord God of heaven we do not have to concern ourselves with curses and recurring mishaps and ills that can make life miserable.

There Is One and Only True God

True happiness in this world comes when you make the decision to obey and worship the one and only true God—the self-described *"I AM"* (Exodus 3:14). God asserts His identity to His children as He explains to them His role in their lives: *"You are my witnesses," declares the Lord, "and my servant whom I have chosen, so that you may know and believe me and understand that I am he. Before me, no other God was formed, nor will there be one after me. I, even I, am the Lord, and apart from me there is no savior"* (Isaiah 43:10-11).

> *True happiness in this world comes when you make the decision to obey and worship the one and only true God*

The Bible contrasts Christ's role in our lives to the role that Satan play in people's lives. The scripture compares Satan to a thief: *"The thief comes only to steal and kill and destroy; I have come that you may have life, and have it to the full"* (John 10:10, NIV). The devil and his demons, through sects, occults, secret societies, idolatries and magic may give you temporary relief and happiness, but these will not last. In the final analysis, Satan destroys and takes as many people as he can, sometimes several generations of people out of one family. Jesus Christ, the Son of God, is the foundation on which we should build our lives. Christ declares, *"I am the way and the truth and the life . . ."* (John 14:6). And the Bible confirms this about Christ: *"In him was life, and that life was the light of men. The light shines in the darkness, but the darkness has not understood it"* (John 1:4-5).

I advise you to calculate well before choosing the God you will serve in life. Christ has made a promise to those who follow Him: *"Come to me, all you who are weary and burdened, and I will give you rest. Take my yoke upon you and learn from me, for I am gentle and humble in heart, and you will find rest for your souls. For my yoke is easy and my burden is light"* (Matthew 11:28-30, NIV). Christ has the authority to make this promise because following His resurrection, He told His disciples, *"All authority in heaven and on earth has been given to me"* (Matthew 28:18, NIV). Further Christ says, *"I am Alpha and Omega, the beginning and the end, the first and the last"* (Revelation 22:13, NIV).

> *I advise you to calculate well before choosing the God you will serve in life.*

When you put your full weight on the promises and teachings of Christ, you will be able to stand against the whims and threats of Satan in any given situation. I am reminded of the story of Polycarp, the bishop of Smyrna, and the last survivor of persons who knew the apostles. Polycarp was an old man when he was arrested and brought to the amphitheater in Smyrna. Before an amphitheater full of spectators, the proconsul offered Polycarp his freedom if he denied the Lord Jesus Christ. Polycarp replied, *"I have served Him for eighty years, and He has never disappointed me; how can I deny and blaspheme against my King? He is MY SAVIOR. I'm still a Christian"* (The Church in History, 45). What a testimony to remember about a faithful Christian!

"Humility and the fear of the Lord bring wealth and honor and life" (Proverbs 22:4, NIV). Choose to worship the only true God.

After serving and worshipping the only true God for his whole life, Joshua declared to the children of Israel:

> *"But if serving the Lord seems undesirable to you, then choose for yourselves this day whom you will serve, whether the gods your forefathers served beyond the River, or the gods of the Amorites, in whose land you are living. But as for me and my household, we will serve the Lord"* (Joshua 24:15, NIV).

David, the king of Israel served and worshipped the only true and eternal God his whole life. He admonishes us, *"Taste and see that the Lord is good; blessed is the man who takes refuge in him"* (Joshua 24:15).

Calculate to Choose the Right Career

There is an old saying, *"The job makes the man."* The person who chooses the right profession, that is, a profession that is honorable and suitable for the individual has made a good choice. It makes becoming successful in life much less daunting when you are working in a profession that you like and one that gives you satisfaction. However, your love and enjoyment you have for your job today may take a different turn tomorrow. Circumstances can change on a job in various ways, a new management can take over; the job description can change; a supervisor or manager can change the dynamics of the workplace. Yet, whatever the situation, we need to work. I am reminded of a comment from *Voltaire,* one of my favorite French philosophers, and essayist from the Enlightenment Period. Known for his philosophical sport, defense of civil liberties (especially freedom of religion and free trade), and wit, the Frenchman comments: *"Work saves us from three great evils: boredom, vice, and need."*

> *"The job makes the man."*

People usually cannot build a successful life without a job. Some people who live miserable lives in societies around the world are persons who are not working or persons who are not working steadily. Then there are those who work, but they do not make enough money to build a successful life for themselves nor their families. In too many instances, these people have not made the appropriate calculations regarding employment.

Since most of us are destined to work for the duration of our eligible working years, making the right calculations for job preparation and job choice is crucial. Take inventory of yourself:

- What are your negative attributes?
- What is your access of your attitude and character? Do you like dealing with the general public?
- Do you primarily prefer working with others or working alone?
- What do you like or enjoy doing?
- How are your language skills?
- Are you adequately trained for what you enjoy and like doing?
- What time of day or night do you prefer to begin work?
- Are you willing to invest the time and energy to become properly trained for what you want to do?
- Are you healthy?
- Does your appearance attract others to you, or does it repel others from you?
- How do you like to dress for work?
- Are you willing to come in at entry level on a job and work your way up?

Knowing this information about yourself will not limit you; rather, the information creates a profile that will be helpful as you calculate your next job or may even the career that will serve you for a lifetime. You certainly do not want to select a job that is parallel to who you are, what you like, and what you have the skills to do. The construction of your life can become greatly flawed if you make these mistakes. Know that your job choice is one of the weight-bearing walls of your life.

Few things are more disheartening than to go to work everyday to a job that is not satisfying. There are people who have jobs that pay them well and offer wonderful benefits, but they are miserable despite these attributes of the employment. The truth is, you cannot build a successful life in its entirety if you are not happy with your job. An eight-hour work-day takes up about one-third of our lives. That is a big chunk of time to be unhappy. The problem about being unhappy with your job is that the unhappiness is not limited to the hours we are working. That unhappiness spills over into the time you spend dreading going to work the next day and counting the hours on the weekend before it is time to return to work. How miserable! To avoid this fiasco, seek God's favor and blessing for your job choice. *"A man can receive only what is given to him from heaven"* (John 3:27). In other words, individuals achieve the greatest happiness in their employment if they receive it from heaven. Again, seek God to direct and help you to discover what He wants you to accomplish in this world. You can pray this simple prayer: Dear Lord, please guide and direct me toward a career choice that will make use of the special gifts you have given me, and direct me to use these gifts in ways that will glorify you. Please help me to develop a good work ethic so that I will be obedient to you according to Paul's instructions to the Colossians: *"Whatever you do, work at it with all your heart, as working for the Lord, not for men, since you know that you will receive an inheritance from the Lord as a reward. It is the Lord Christ you are serving"* (Colossians 3:23-24, NIV).

> *Know that your job choice is one of the weight-bearing walls of your life.*

Calculate to Choose the Right Spouse

Though the primary theme of this book is not about marriage, I am compelled to give this subject some special attention. Why? Because marriage is an important part of living and it impacts greatly whether or not one builds a successful life with or without the existence of this kind of relationship in your personal world.

When I was younger I thought I would be married when I reached twenty- two years old. But by the time I reached the age of twenty-two, I discovered that I had a lot of calculations to make in the light of God's Word.

- What was God's purpose for me?
- What was God's destiny for me?
- What kind of woman should I choose to become my wife?
- How many children would we want to have?
- What should be our dreams for them?
- What kind of legacy would I want to leave for my descendents?

When I finished listing these calculations that had to be made, I knew that then was not the right time for me to marry.

Marriage is a huge part of life as we know it on earth. When the right choices are made, marriage can engender a happiness that can be sustained for a lifetime. But if you fail to make the right choice for a spouse, that failure is one of the most devastating failures that people experience. A miserable marriage has a domino effect—a miserable marriage produces a miserable family; a miserable family produces miserable adults and children; miserable people create a miserable environment, and a miserable environment produces a miserable life. And where misery lives, happiness cannot dwell. It is impossible for the two to co-exist.

Be careful not to fall into the traps that Satan sets to capture you by the foolish desires of your heart. It is highly possible that you easily will miss the purpose and destiny God has in mind for you if you enter into marriage with the wrong person. Remember, I have made the point clear before that God has a divine plan for every person, family, nation, country, and continent. And marriage is a part of the divine plan that He has for every person. Therefore, seek the will of God for your marriage. And know this, every marriage outside of the will of God will be problematic and unhappy. It is better to take your time and make the necessary calculations when choosing a spouse before launching into a marriage too quickly and ill-advisedly. I will talk about how to make these calculations later in the chapter.

What is marriage?

In my own definition, marriage is a mysterious union of man and woman by God to fulfill His purpose for them upon the earth (Genesis 20:24).

What is the origin of marriage?

Genesis 2:18-24 reveals the origin of marriage as it is ordained by God.

What is the principle objective of marriage?

As we all know, people marry for many reasons:

- They genuinely love one another
- To be happy
- To avoid being lonely
- For financial security
- For companionship
- For sexual fulfillment
- For social acceptance

For whatever reason people choose to marry, it is important to know why God instituted the marital relationship. My research of the scriptures revealed that God unites a man and women so that together they can fulfill God's purpose that is based on their relationship as husband and wife. Let's look at some marriages that we can read about in the scriptures.

Adam and Eve

The purpose of Adam and Eve's marriage was to be fruitful and multiply, to replenish the earth, to subdue it, and exercise power over everything on the earth and under the sea (Genesis 1:28).

Abraham and Sarah

The purpose of the Abraham and Sarah's marriage was for Abraham to be the father of a great Hebrew nation through the birth of his son Isaac (Genesis 12:5).

Isaac and Rebecca

The purpose of Isaac and Rebekah's marriage was to birth Jacob (whose name was changed to Israel) who would later become the father of the twelve tribes (Genesis 24:1-64).

Jacob and Rachael

The purpose of Jacob and Rachael's marriage was to conceive Joseph who delivered the house of his father, Jacob, from a great famine, and it is through Joseph that promises God made to Abraham were fulfilled (Genesis 15:1-15 and 29:15-30, and chapters 43, 47).

Amram and Jochebed

The purpose of Amram and Jochebed's marriage was to birth Aaron, Miriam, and Moses from whom God would raise up Moses to be the greatest prophet among the children of Israel (Exodus 2:1 and Numbers 26:59).

Boaz and Ruth

The purpose of Boaz and Ruth's marriage was for them to conceive Obed, the father of Jesse who would beget David who would become the shepherd boy who rose to become the king of Israel, a prophet, a great warrior, and psalmist of Israel (Ruth chapters 3 and 4).

King Ahasuerus and Esther

The purpose of King Ahasuerus and Esther's marriage was

to put Esther in a place and position to deliver the Jewish nation from a conspiracy designed to destroy them (Esther 2:1-18 and chapters 3-10).

Zacharias and Elizabeth

The purpose of Zacharias and Elizabeth's marriage was for them to conceive John in the couple's old age to demonstrate the power of God through this miracle of birth, and the baby would become the forerunner of Jesus and he would baptize the Lord (Luke 1:5-25, 36-80 and Matthew 3:13-17).

Joseph and Mary

The purpose of Joseph and Mary's marriage was to serve as the earthly parents of the Lord Jesus Christ, the savior of humanity (Matthew 1:18-25).

Thus, God has several purposes for marriage, the principle one I believe, is for the man and woman to collaborate with one another to accomplish God's purpose through them as husband and wife. Many precious teachings from different Bible teachers on marriage have revealed to us that God's purpose for marriage is to reflect His image (Genesis 1:26-27), for the couple to multiply (Genesis 1:28), to manage the earth (Genesis 1:28), to support and complete one another (Genesis 2:18) and to be an example of Christ and the church (Ephesians 5:31-32). This collaboration for the fulfillment of God's purpose is based on three points in the life of the couple.

Worship and Service to God

God wants to use every marriage for His service one way of the other. He established marriage so that man and woman can worship and serve Him through their union as husband and wife. In most cases this union will be blessed with offspring who will be raised to glorify God and to perpetuate the kingdom of God on earth until Christ returns to the earth to claim those who are His.

Construction and Success of Husbands and Wives' Lives in the Marriage Covenant

God instituted marriage because He said that it is not good for man to be alone (Genesis 2:18). Therefore, God made the wife to be a helper to her husband, to assist him throughout their lives together. In so doing, good wives aid in helping their husbands grow spiritually and to be successful as they work together to construct the lives they live on earth.

Service to Society and the World

God established marriage so that together a husband and wife can be profitable to society and sometimes even profitable to the world by their service and good works. For example, look at the way Amram and Jochebed served God by raising Moses as a son who would leave his footprints on his native land and the world. Another married couple to consider is Elkanah and Hannah. Their service and commitment to God influenced them to raise Samuel so that he, also, would leave indelible marks of service, obedience, and leadership as great examples for the world to follow.

Preparation for Marriage

One reason some marriages have serious problems is because one or both persons in the relationship failed to prepare one way or the other to be a good spouse. To succeed in anything in life, we need to prepare for it. Preparation is one of the earmarks of success.

I discovered that God Almighty, the creator of the universe, does not do anything without preparation. God took 430 years to groom the Israelites to become a nation. He took 4,000 years to prepare for the birth, ministry, death, resurrection, and ascension of the Lord Jesus Christ (from the fall of Adam to the birth of the Messiah). God has taken more than 6,000 years to prepare the Christian family, and up to this point He has taken more than 7,000 years to prepare for the New Jerusalem and eternal life for His children.

Since God allows plenty of time for preparation for His undertakings, how much more should we take time to prepare for marriage? A successful marriage equals a successful life. Though there might be some exceptions, preparation for marriage should be dealt with in all of the important domains of your life—spiritual, family, psychological, emotional, material, financial, and moral. From personal experience, serious talking and/or counseling is a good first step when preparing for marriage. Most importantly, however, it is necessary for the couple to have a love and commitment to do God's will before they marry. Pray that God will order your steps and see you through years of loving and respecting one another as husband and wife.

The Right Time

There is a cliché that says, *"Timing is everything."* One important calculation you should make concerning marriage is timing. *"To everything there is a season, and a time to every purpose under the heaven"* (Ecclesiastes 3:1, KJV). You should calculate when the right time is for you to begin to consider marriage and when the right time is for you to actually get married. Seek God's answer to the appropriate time for you to marry.

How to Choose Your Spouse

If you think you want to marry, or if you know you want to marry, there are some steps that you can take that will increase your possibility of choosing the appropriate spouse. Let me make this clear, without a special direction, leading or approval from God, you must take quality time to make some calculations before making up your mind about who to select as a marriage partner. Let's talk about some sage advice.

- **Pray fervently.** As you pray to ask God to send you a spouse, submit yourself to the directions that God gives concerning marriage. First and foremost, keep this message of God in mind:

    "Do not be yoked together with unbelievers. For what do righteousness and wickedness have in common? Or what fellowship can light have with darkness? What harmony is there between Christ and Belial [a demon]? What does a believer have in common with an unbeliever? What

agreement is there between the temple of God and idols? For we are the temple of the living God. As God has said, "I will live with them and walk among them, and I will be their God, and they will be my people. Therefore come out from them and be separate, says the Lord (II Corinthians 6:14-17, NIV).

- **Seek to know the purpose, plan, and will of God for your life.** When you have this information for your own life, then you know to seek a spouse who shares the same vision. Otherwise, there will in all likelihood be problems. He who does not fulfill the will of God for his life will be unhappy. Samson failed to do the perfect will of God when he did not heed his parents' advice for whom to choose for a wife. He married Delilah who did not share his spiritual vision, a decision that brought Samson much misery and a decision he lived to regret (Judges chapters 13-15).

- **Identify your positive and negative traits.** The attention here should be to focus on your negative attributes. Are these negatives in your character potential deal-breakers for a marriage? Certainly you should work diligently to improve and correct these faults. You do not want to enter a marriage carrying liabilities. Compatibility and completeness are two good attributes that should be at work in a couple who is contemplating marriage. However, *couples should understand that no two people are exactly alike.* Despite differences, however, couples should be able to complete one another in order to achieve love and harmony in the relationship.

- **Allow a sufficient amount of time and the Holy Spirit to reveal to you the person you should marry.** This means you need to take your time and not rush into making the relationship serious before its time. You need to discover the "real person." What is this person's spiritual background and standing? Where and how does God fit into the person's life. Is the person emotionally and psychologically sound? Is the person materialistic? How does this person manage finances? How does this person handle and deal with problems? Is this person selfish or giving? Is there anything in this person's past that needs to be discussed? How do the two of you feel about one another's family and friends? What is the person's short term and long term goals?These are just some of the questions that need clearly defined answers before you can make the decision that this is the person God intends for you to marry.

- **Decide whether or not you can handle the strengths and weaknesses of a potential spouse.** We seldom have problems with a person's strengths. It is a person's weaknesses that give us trouble. For example, if you like your surroundings orderly and neat, can you handle someone who is disorderly and messy? Unless you can satisfactorily negotiate a compromise on this issue over time it can become a serious problem in the marriage.

- **Observe whether or not your potential spouse has the makings of being a good parent.** Listen and take note of how your potential spouse feels about children and acts around them. Will he or she be a strong disciplinarian or a permissive parent? Your children will be the legacy you leave on earth. It is so much easier to raise godly children if parents can work together toward the same spiritual goal for their children.

- **Make sure the will of God intends for you to marry the person you have chosen to be your spouse.** God finds all kinds of ways to reveal messages to you, especially when you earnestly seek the truth. He may choose to reveal or confirm His will to you about marriage in any of the following ways:

    Through the Word of God. The first step that can help you to know the will of God concerning marriage is the Word of God. Any relationship that is not acceptable by the commandments of God or contrary to the moral laws of God found in His Word is not of God. Do not marry an unbeliever, someone who does not worship or serve God or someone who is not living for God and trying to please God. Do not marry a man or woman who is married and trying to leave the husband or wife to marry you. Again, I am reminded of the scripture that says, *"Do not be yoked* *together with unbelievers. For what do righteousness and wickedness have in common? Or what fellowship can light have with darkness"* (I Corinthians 6: 14, NIV)?

Through expressions of real love. There is a difference between real love and lust. Lust is an intense or unbridled sexual desire, an obsessive sexual craving or desire for what is forbidden. How can you know if your attraction to someone is real love or lust? Concentrate on getting to know the person's likes, dislikes, interests, aspirations, and so forth. And by all means, avoid having pre-marital sex. Give yourself sometime to see if what you are feeling is real love or the attraction that comes from meeting someone new, different, and exciting. It is difficult to tell the difference between real love and lust if you are engaged in a sexual relationship. The Bible condemns the practice of pre-marital sex. Read the beautiful love story of Jacob and Rachel in Genesis 29:18-30. Notice the purity of their relationship during the period of courtship.

Through circumstances orchestrated by God. When Moses fled from Egypt and sat down by the well, where he drove away the shepherds who were preventing the daughters of Jethro from fetching water for their flock, later the Bible states, *"And Moses was content to dwell with the man [Jethro]: and he gave Moses Zipporah his daughter"* to marry (Exodus 2:21).

Another example of circumstances being orchestrated by God for two people to marry is seen in the case of Joseph after he interpreted the dream of Pharaoh in Egypt. The Bible states, *"And Pharaoh called Joseph's name Zaphnathpaaneah; and he gave him to wife Asenath the daughter of Potipherah priest of On. And Joseph went out over all the land of Egypt'* (Genesis 41:45).

Should you consider similar circumstances as the will of God for you to marry someone? The answer is left for you to discover. Not all circumstances of help or services are meant by God for people to get married. Therefore, consider some of them just as a service or help from God and do not put yourself under bondages and blame them on situations. Again, let time and the Holy Spirit show you if you have to fall in love with such a person to marry him/her.

Through signs. After Abraham made his servant swear not to take a wife for his son Isaac among the Canaanites, the Bible says, *"Then the servant took ten of his master's camels and left, taking with him all kinds of good things from his master. He set out for Aram Naharaim and made his way to the town of Nahor. He had the camels kneel down near the well outside the town; it was toward evening, the time the women go out to draw water. Then he prayed, "O Lord, God of my master Abraham, give me success today, and show kindness to my master Abraham. See, I am standing beside this spring, and the daughters of the townspeople are coming out to draw water. May it be that when I say to a girl, 'Please let down your jar that I may have a drink,' and she says,*

> *'Drink, and I'll water your camels too'--let her be the one you have chosen for your servant Isaac. By this I will know that you have shown kindness to my master." Before he had finished praying, Rebekah came out with her jar on her shoulder. She was the daughter of Bethuel son of Milcah, who was the wife of Abraham's brother Nahor. The girl was very beautiful, a virgin; no man had ever lain with her. She went down to the spring, filled her jar and came up again. The servant hurried to meet her and said, "Please give me a little water from your jar. "Drink, my lord," she said, and quickly lowered the jar to her hands and gave him a drink. After she had given him a drink, she said, "I'll draw water for your camels too, until they have finished drinking. "So she quickly emptied her jar into the trough, ran back to the well to draw more water, and drew enough for all his camels. Without saying a word, the man watched her closely to learn whether or not the LORD had made his journey successful. When the camels had finished drinking, the man took out a gold nose ring weighing a beka and two gold bracelets weighing ten shekels. Then he asked, "Whose daughter are you? Please tell me, is there room in your father's house for us to spend the night? "She answered him, "I am the daughter of Bethuel, the son that Milcah bore to Nahor. "And she added, "We have plenty of straw and fodder, as well as room for you to spend the night. "Then the man bowed down and worshiped the Lord, saying, "Praise be to the Lord, the God of my master Abraham, who has not abandoned his kindness and faithfulness to my master"* (Genesis 24:1-27).

Cleary the servant of Abraham asked God for a sign to know His will about what woman to choose to be the wife of Isaac. Therefore, you may also ask God for a sign to know the will of God regarding your choice for a marriage partner. However, be open for other ways the Holy Spirit may use to confirm the will of God to you.

God uses many ways to speak to His children. You may come to know the will of God's choice for a spouse by the gifts of manifestations of the Holy Spirit: the gift of discernment, word of knowledge and prophesy (I Corinthians 12:1-11). Again, I would like to warn you to be real with people and yourself in order to be sure God is talking to you. Be careful and do not let the devil fool you into destruction. While you are in search of your spouse, remember not all feelings and revelations will come from God; it may be from your own flesh or the devil. Devote a lot of time in prayer and wait on God to lead and help you make the right decision.

Three Kinds of Marriages

There are many different kinds of marriages based upon cultural, regional, continental, racial, and ethnic backgrounds. Sometimes, people combine elements of various marital traditions and create a unique style for their nuptials.

The Traditional Marriage

The traditional marriage is exercised according to the traditions and cultures of every race, tribe, region or country. I will suggest to you as a Christian that you plan a wedding ceremony that is not filled with worldly elements and activities that dishonor the marriage ceremony and dishonor God.

The Civil Marriage

The civil marriage ceremony is usually conducted in the office of a justice of the peace. There is nothing wrong with the civil marriage, but I advise you to do more than a civil marriage. Marriage is such an important part of your life that it should be celebrated in a special way after all. Consider having an ecclesiastical marriage as a Christian to commit your marriage into the hands of God.

The Ecclesiastical Marriage

The ecclesiastical marriage is a marriage ceremony that is base upon biblical principles from the Old and New Testaments, and it is usually performed by a minister or priest. As a Christian, your desire should be to marry according to the Bible or the Word of God. I understand that getting married by a minister does not guarantee the success of a marriage. However the decision to plan an ecclesiastical ceremony means you believe in the power of God and that you commit your marriage into the full control of God through His power, His Spirit and His Word.

Obstacles of Marriage

Since I started studying the dynamics of the marital relationship, I realize that there are a number of obstacles that will occur between married couples or two individuals in relationship. Since we are human, we are prone to make mistakes, and sometimes it is these mistakes that cause problems.

Incredulity

Let me reaffirm that the fear of God should be the foundation of every child of God's marriage, and this fear or reverence for God should be exercised in marriage. If you properly fear and obey God, you will be willing to marry for the right reasons. You will not allow wrong and selfish reasons such as the desires of your flesh dictate this major decision to marry. When you fail to obey God about whom to marry, you are certain to harvest the dire consequences. Be careful, take your time, wait and listen to God, and let Him order your steps. Do not resist the will of God.

Money and Material Possessions

A second obstacle to some marriages concerns money and material possessions. As I stated in the preface, materials, money, beauty and fame do not guarantee success and happiness in life, even though these may be part of a successful life. Ironically, these may be absent from your life, yet you can know success without them.

With this truth in mind, I encourage you to not allow the meager material or financial disposition of someone to prevent you from marrying. I am not encouraging you to marry an irresponsible person, but keep in mind that not everybody who is poor or going through some challenges of life is irresponsible, and not worth marrying. For bad things do happen to good people. Sometimes there are extenuating circumstances that have impacted one's financial and material standing. The most important things you have to check and consider are the person's relationship with God, values, characters, attitudes, smart and hardworking, and potentials, which can create or produce the dream husband or wife and the fulfilled life, purpose and destiny you have always wanted and expected.

The Origin of the Person or Family Background

To consider the origin of a person is to look into the family, race, tribe, village, state, region, nationality, and country of the individual. Sometimes cross-cultural marriages face special issues and problems. However, these problems or any problem can be mastered if the will of God is for two people from different cultures marry. As long as God agrees to the marriage, He will surely order your steps and help you to have a happy, fruitful marriage.

Parents and Other Relatives

Parents can play an important role in their children's marriage. Many of them assume the right to express their opinion, advice, and suggestions about their child's marriage. However, let me advise that parents' input should be done according to the Word of God. That is, their contributions should be godly, based on Christian values, and guided by the truth of the Word of God. I am not saying your parents have to be Christians before they can have a say regarding your marriage, but make sure the advice you take from them is in line with the truth in the Word of God. Sometimes parents may tend to give ungodly advice to their children that deviates from the will of God. Yes, the Bible does tell children to obey their parents, but there is a condition that governs this command. The scripture says, *"Children, obey your parents in the Lord, for this is right"* (Ephesians 6:1, KJV). Remember, as I have referenced before, Samson did not listen to the godly advice his parents gave him about whom to choose for a wife. The end result is that he chose to marry the wrong person and this decision drastically alter his life. (Judges chapters 14, 15 and 16).

To parents, I say, talk to your children about the appropriate choice for a mate long before the child reaches the age when marriage is a consideration and possibility. This is a way to safeguard children against making bad choices in the persons they choose to date. In fact, encourage them not to date anyone whom they would not consider for marriage. Also, train children to want to please God. By establishing this mind-set early, you may very well be saving your children from bucketfuls of heartache that people experience who did not get such sage advice from their parents.

Friends

Is also a common practice to allow your friends to deviate you from the will of God for your marriage. Do not allow friends to influence you in directions that take you away from God's plan for your life. Often friends mean well, but if they are pointing you and your decisions about marriage in a wrong direction, tell them, "Thanks, but no thanks."

On the other hand, God can use friends at times to deliver you from wrong choices. Therefore, be sober-minded and seek God about the advice you receive from friends about your relationship with others and marriage. The Holy Spirit will help you recognize the good and right advice you receive from friends.

Beauty

Naturally, everybody is attracted to beauty. Every man would like to marry the most beautiful woman in the world, and every woman would like to marry the handsomest man in the world. We see this natural desire in the life of Jacob: *Laban had two daughters; the name of the older was Leah, and the name of the younger was Rachel. Leah had weak eyes, but Rachel was lovely in form, and beautiful. Jacob was in love with Rachel and [Jacob tells Laban], "I'll work for you seven years in return for your younger daughter Rachel"* (Genesis 29: 16-18, NIV). Jacob loved Rachel so much that the seven years of work seemed but a few days to him (Genesis 29:20).

After the seven years passed, Laban tricked Jacob and gave him Leah for his bride instead of Rachel. When Jacob discovered that Laban, deceived him (verse 23), Jacob agreed to work seven more years for Laban to consent for Rachel to marry him. Jacob was captivated by the beauty of the younger daughter of Laban. Read this amazing story in Geneses 29: 14-30).

There is nothing wrong with marrying a beautiful woman, but do not let beauty lead you to marry the wrong person. To marry a beautiful woman or a handsome man can be an added blessing, but do not let beauty be the center and fundamental measure of your choice. Beauty can do little to help you to build a successful life and maintain it.

Obviously Rachel had other attributes that attracted Jacob, though it was her beauty that first caught his attention. Do not base the choice of your husband or wife on beauty alone; look beyond that. Be mindful that there are some beautiful people in the world who have no substance to their character and attitude. *"Like a gold ring in a pig's snout is a beautiful woman who shows no discretion"* (Proverbs 11: 22).

What it Takes to be Successful

Do you remember from where we have come? We have just had a somewhat extensive discussion about the calculations you need to make in your life in order to select a good mate for marriage, one who will compliment you spiritually and in other ways so that the two of you can build a successful life together. Now let's talk about what it takes to build a successful life. I have addressed the use of your faith, intelligence, knowledge, wisdom, talents, natural and spiritual gifts, charisma, money, and so forth to achieve personal success, but let's go deeper.

Let's review what I call Jesus' great instructions to His disciples as He talked to them about counting up the cost:

> *"Suppose one of you wants to build a tower. Will he not first sit down and estimate the cost to see if he has enough money to complete it? For if he lays the foundation and is not able to finish it, everyone who sees it will ridicule him, saying, "This fellow began to build and was not able to finish." Or suppose a king is about to go to war against another king. Will he not first sit down and consider whether he is able with ten thousand men to oppose the*

one coming against him with twenty thousand? If he is not able, he will send a delegation while the other is still a long way off and will ask for terms of peace". In the same way, any of you who does not give up everything he has cannot be my disciple. Salt is good, but if it loses its saltiness, how can it be made salty again? It is fit neither for the soil nor for the manure pile; it is thrown out. He who has ears to hear, let him hear (Luke 14:28-35).

In this passage of scripture, Christ gives three scenarios of real-life situations in which calculations need to be done before people venture into tasks—calculations to decide whether or not to build a tower, calculations to decide whether or not to go to war, and calculations to decide whether or not a person will decide to become a follower of Christ. These are good examples to demonstrate the kind of calculations you should take time to make to see if you have what it takes to build a successful life. Your task is to calculate based on scripture whether or not you have what it takes to be successful in these areas:

- The plan
- The money
- The land
- The laborers
- The materials
- The foundation
- The endurance

The Plan

Your plan is the method by which you plan to accomplish

your goal to build a successful life. As you make your plans, keep in mind that the chief architect is God. Like Abraham looked for a city whose builder and maker was God (Hebrews 11:8-10), you, also have to look to God to be the chief architect of your life.

The Money

Money or some form of it is important in every society. On one hand, the scripture says there are instances when *"money is the answer for everything"* (Ecclesiastes 10:19, NIV). But also the Bible warns us about money when it is not viewed from the right perspective: *"For the love of money is a root of all kinds of evil. Some people, eager for money, have wandered from the faith and pierced themselves with many griefs"* (I Timothy 6:10, NIV). When you become engaged in building a successful life, there will be times when money will not be plentiful. Do not get so eager for money that you practice unscrupulous schemes to get it. The Lord will provide for your monetary needs in due time, especially if you remain true to Him in all your efforts. He will direct your steps to where to find money, or He will see that the money you need comes to you. The money may not come when you want it, but it will surely come on time.

The Land

To build a house or tower, you need land or a place. One reason some people are unable to build successful lives is because they are not at a location God has ordained for them. You may be at a place where everybody else is succeeding and the location maybe a good location, but if the place is not where God wants you, you will not experience total success.

Let me make an analogy here. Not all plants grow equally on the same land or in the same soil. A piece of land may be well suited for one plant and may not be good for another. Sometime a plant that is not planted on compatible land will encounter difficulties in development and may even die. The scripture likens the person who delights in the law of God to a plant: *"He is like a tree planted by streams of water, which yields its fruit in season and whose leaf does not wither. Whatever he does prospers"* (Psalms 1:3, NIV). In the next verse the ungodly is compared to a plant as well: "[The wicked] are like chaff that the wind blows away" (Psalm 1:4, NIV).

The story of Abraham fits perfectly here. The land where Abraham achieved success was the land of Canaan.

The LORD had said to Abram (Abraham), *"Leave your country, your people and your father's household and go to the land I will show you. I will make you into a great nation and I will bless you; I will make your name great, and you will be a blessing. I will bless those who bless you, and whoever curses you I will curse; and all peoples on earth will be blessed through you." So Abram left, as the LORD had told him; and Lot went with him. Abram was seventy-five years old when he set out from Haran. He took his wife Sarai (Sarah), his nephew Lot, all the possessions they had accumulated and the people they had acquired in Haran, and they set out for the land of Canaan, and they arrived there* (Genesis 12:1-5).

Abraham had already proved his faithfulness to God when God approached this son of Nahor and gave him a command to leave his father's house and his country. Upon Abraham immediate obedience to God, the obedient servant set the wheels in motion for God to bless him in a special way. God made several promises to Abraham—that he would be the father of a great nation, that he would be blessed, that his name would become great in the land, and everybody on earth will be blessed through him. Certainly God kept all of His promises to Abraham to the magnitude that no one could ever dream.

I advise you to pray and ask God where He wants you to stay to build your successful life. Seek to know the church where God wants you to worship and serve Him. Ask Him where He wants you to earn a living as you work on building a successful life. Know that you have a Canaan land just like Abraham and you need God's instructions to help you find the territory you will inhabit to build a successful life.

The Laborers

The scriptures have much to say about laborers. The Bible comments that there are few laborers (Matthew 9:37) even though the harvest is plentiful. It speaks of the double honor that is due church elders who labor in the word and doctrine, and says the laborer is worthy of his pay (I Timothy 5:17-18). It tells us to work diligently in life for there is no work that can be done in the grave (Ecclesiastes 9:10). Work is so honorable with God that He says a man who will not work should not eat (II Thessalonians 3:10). The Lord gives us permission to enjoy the fruits of our labor (I Corinthians 9:7-14). Therefore, the Lord endorses our decision to work smart and hard to build a life that is successful and to build a life that glorifies the Father in heaven.

The Materials

Though we have already talked about the following subjects, I want to reinforce them into your spirit. To build a spiritual house or tower, you need spiritual materials, and some of these materials are spiritual:

> **Prayer.** Prayer is essential for the success of the life of a child of God. If you want to build a successful life, you need to be a praying person. You have to work on having a successful prayer life for this is essential for you to accomplish your goals.
>
> In the Bible the children of God who succeeded both physically and spiritually were praying people. Prayer puts you in communion with God, and being in communion with God enables the Power and the Spirit of God to be in action in your life and your affairs.
>
> To build a successful life, you have to pray and commend all your ways into the hands of God, asking Him for direction, protection, and authority over any plans the devil has to thwart your desire to fulfill your purpose and destiny. The Bible admonishes, *"Ask and it will be given to you; seek and you will find; knock and the door will be opened to you"* (Matthew 7:7, NIV). *Therefore, you are free to make your requests known to God. And a final reminder, "Do not be anxious about anything, but in everything, by prayer and petition, with thanksgiving, present your requests to God"* (Philippians 4:6, NIV).

Fasting. When you fast according to the will of God, *"Then your light will break forth like the dawn, and your healing will quickly appear; then your righteousness will go before you, and the glory of the LORD will be your rear guard. Then you will call, and the LORD will answer; you will cry for help, and he will say: Here am I"* (Isaiah 58:1-7).

Again, fasting is a vital tool you need to build a life in which you can enjoy success. As degrees of your success become more and more evident, the light of God's grace in your life will break forth. Therefore, if you add fasting to your prayer life, your destiny will come forth.

Sanctification. By nature humans are sinful beings: *"For all have sinned and fall short of the glory of God"* (Romans 3:23). You cannot build a successful life by your own power. You need the help of the Spirit of the Most high God (Zachariah 4:6). When the Spirit of God is infused in your plans, the outcome of your success reaches far beyond what your imagination, intelligence, wisdom, and abilities can conceive. Just as the glory of God went before the children of Israel directing them as they were traveling in the wilderness, the glory of God will lead you the same way as you travel the road of life seeking success and satisfaction.

While your life is under construction, keep it pure. Notice that when the children of Israel sinned in the desert, the glory of God departed from them, and it was at that time their enemies were able to overtake them. Why? Because when the children of Israel fell short of God's glory, they were punished. As you construct your life, be sure to separate yourself from sin in every form and manifestation. Do your best to keep your life sanctified and clean by the help of the Holy Spirit and the blood of the Lord Jesus. Peter admonishes Christians to be this way: *"As children, not fashioning yourselves according to the former lusts in your ignorance. But as He who have called you is holy, so you be holy in all manner of conversation; because it is written, 'Be holy, for I am holy"* (I Peter 1:14-16, NIV). II Timothy 2:19 says, *"Nevertheless, God's solid foundation stands firm, sealed with this inscription: The Lord knows those who are His. And, let every one that named the name of Christ depart from iniquity"* (NIV). 5:19).

The Foundation

When building any kind of construction, it is imperative to build a firm foundation. If the foundation of a building is not solid or well built, it will affect the sturdiness and stability of the structure. Over time, it will collapse sooner or latter. I have heard about buildings that started crumbling progressively a few weeks after their inaugurations, and investigations revealed that the foundations were not solid. The art of construction affirms that you need a strong foundation to have a strong building that will last.

It is one thing to build a house, and another thing for the house to resist natural disasters. Likewise, it is one thing to build a successful life, and it is another thing for your success to be able to resist and survive the challenges of life.

People who build their lives on evil spirits and powers, and self-assurance discover that they have built their lives on a faulty foundation when the challenges of life assault them sooner or later.

Jesus Christ the Rock

The Lord Jesus Christ declares, *"Therefore, whosoever hears my words and does them, I will compare him to a wise man, who built his house upon a rock. And the rain descended, and the floods came, and the winds blew, and beat upon that house; and it fell not: for it was founded upon a rock. And everyone who hears my sayings and does not do it, will be like a foolish man, who built his house upon the sand: And the rain descended, and the floods came, and the winds blew, and beat upon that house; and it fell and the fall was great"* (Matthew 7:24-27, NIV). In I Corinthians 10:4, the Bible identifies the rock as Christ.

Beloved, if you want to build a life and be successful in every facet of your life until the end, you have to build it on the strongest foundation, on the Lord Jesus Christ, the rock of ages. A life built on God is insured against the challenges of this world that attack it and destroy the happiness in it. Am I saying if you build your life on Christ Jesus, you will not have any problems? No. Nevertheless, when the challenges of this world come, you will surely survive them and keep your joy no matter what happens. Jesus did not say that the rain, the floods and the winds would not come and beat upon that house of the wise man. But despite the assaults of nature upon the wise man's house, the house did not collapse.

The rain, floods, and winds are metaphors for the problems of life that people face from time to time — failure, disappointment, betrayal, sickness, job loss, hopelessness, and death, among others. When some of these life challenges hit you, you will stand and prevail against them. In life, challenges may follow, but only the man or person who builds his house upon the Rock, Jesus Christ of Nazareth, the son of the Living God, the Savior of all men will survive them.

Endurance

According to the *Merriam-Webster English Dictionary*, endurance is the ability to withstand hardship or adversity, especially the ability to sustain a prolonged stressful effort or activity, for example, a marathon runner's endurance. Endurance is also the act or an instance of longsuffering, for example, the endurance of many hardships.

A necessary attribute for building a successful life is endurance. I can recall a personal example of endurance that I have witnessed. A few years ago I visited my maternal family. There is a building that I look forward to seeing each time I go home. As a teenager I was so excited watching the building under construction. When it was finally completed, the building stood out so beautifully at the heart of the city where my grandparents live. I was very excited because I had been watching the building being built for so many years. I do not remember for how many years, but I know that since I was a child. Then I was told that my grandmother who was in her 80's at that time said she was a young adult when the builders started construction. I do not know how many years it took to build and finish that building, but one thing I do know is that it took several decades to start and finish that building. Someone obviously exercised endurance during the time it took to complete construction.

If you want to build a successful life, have lasting success, and come to a good ending of your life, you need to have endurance, the ability to withstand hardship or adversity. As you build your life, some achievements will be easy to achieve—a piece of cake. But there will be some parts of your construction that will require endurance. Construction jobs usually have some surprises. Your goals may take longer to reach than you thought. Satan may throw a wrench or two to clog the smooth flow of your construction. But don't give up. Press on, you will win. *"For everything that was written in the past was written to teach us, so that through endurance and the encouragement of the scriptures we might have hope"* (Romans 15: 4, NIV). Moreover, *"Being strengthened with all power according to his glorious might so that you may have great endurance and patience, and joyfully giving thanks to the Father, who has qualified you to share in the inheritance of the saints in the kingdom of light."* (Colossians 1:11-12).

> *A necessary attribute for building a successful life is endurance.*

PASS IT ON

Lasting success is one that does not end in chaos, mismanagement, dishonesty, cheating, immorality, and shame. If you want to have lasting success, you have to be very careful when you attain your goal. Many people lay aside the

LEADING A SUCCESSFUL LIFE

virtues that allowed them to attain success, and fall into all kinds of immoralities in their attempt to preserve what they have achieved. This kind of living will eventually lead to the dashing of your success. So do not sabotage yourself by leaving the God who brought you to the deep well of success.

Sometimes a successful legacy is not passed from one generation to the next. This occurs when no one was properly groomed to take up the baton to pass on the success. In order for this not to happen to you, pray and ask God to help you choose the right person (s) who will be eager to continue the success that you built during your lifetime. There are noted examples in the scriptures of persons who trained others to continue the work they began. When Moses was leading the children of Israel out of Egypt to the land of Canaan, he trained Joshua to be his successor (Deuteronomy 34: 9). We see the transference of success again from Abraham to Isaac, from Isaac to Jacob, from Jacob to Joseph.

> *Pray and ask God to help you choose the right person (s) who will be eager to continue the success that you built during your lifetime.*

Now that our discussion is drawing to a close, there are several points you should understand clearly.

- You can become somebody even if you are a nobody
- You need to do your homework; investigate your

background so that you really know who you are.
- You should understand that even if your purposes, plans, dreams and heart desires have been broken, God can repair them for you.
- You don't need to worry about your destiny, but be concerned enough to do something about it.
- You need to develop the passion of being useful.
- You need to understand that God uses human beings and things to make you who He wants you to be in this world and to make you do what He wants you to do.
- You know what it takes to build a successful life, what to do to maintain the success, and how to achieve a good ending to your life.
- You understand that if you want to have a lasting success that survives from generation to generation, you have to pass it on by grooming others to carry out your wishes.

Now, GO! Build a successful life (fulfill your destiny); have a lasting success, and may your life finish well or blissfully in Jesus' name. Amen!

About the Author

Willie Yeboah is an Evangelist/Pastor, Author, Poet, Songwriter, Founder and President of Action Jesus Christ International, an interdenominational global evangelism ministry, and Founder of Living God Christian Church International.

For nearly 29 years, both as a preacher and teacher of the Word of God, he has shared the Gospel and power of the Lord Jesus Christ with countless of people through personal evangelism, mass crusades, camp meetings, seminars and many other evangelistic endeavors. People's lives are always touched under the anointing of the Holy Spirit that flows as Pastor Willie Yeboah ministers. His passion for soul winning is always seen through his daily activities, which always target the accomplishment of the great commission.

www.ingramcontent.com/pod-product-compliance
Lightning Source LLC
Chambersburg PA
CBHW072231290426
44111CB00012B/2045